On Dreams

Edited by Arlene Kramer Richards

On Dreams

**Edited by
Arlene
Kramer
Richards**

IPBOOKS.net

International Psychoanalytic Books (IPBooks)
New York • www.IPBooks.net

International Psychoanalytic Books (IPBooks), Queens, NY

Online at: www.IPBooks.net

Cover painting: Henri Rousseau, The Sleeping Gypsy, 1897.

Cover and interior book design by Kathy Kovacic, Blackthorn Studio

ISBN: 978-1-956864-69-4

CONTENTS

At Last: Dreams for Controversial Discussions

Dreams Within Dreams

Eugene Mahon

(2002). *Psychoanalytic Study of the Child,* 57:118–130 (www.pep-web.org/search.php?volume=57&journal=psc.)

The concept of a dream-within-a-dream is studied intensively. The illusion created by the dream work portrays one portion of a dream enacted within the envelope of another. Freud (1900) emphasized that the function of placing a piece of reality in a dream within a dream is an attempt to rob it of its significance and obliterate it. However, he seemed curiously disinterested in the fact that segmentation of a dream text into two seemingly discrete fragments does offer a dream investigator the opportunity to explore he dynamic relationship between the two fragments and the multiple meanings of the illusion created during sleep. In this study the linkage between the two parts of the dream sequence is highlighted. While Freud's intuition is corroborated, his lack of interest in the duality of the dream events is puzzling, as if he believed that only the dream within a dream is meaningful and the complementary and contextual dream sequence can be ignored. This paper suggests that both portions of the dream within a dream are significant, the one helping to explicate the other as the free-associative process of dream interpretation gives equal democratic time to both.

Why would a dreamer immersed in the illusion of dream imagine that he has awakened but in fact go on dreaming a "new dream" so that on actual awakening his experience will seem to have been a dream within a dream? If one pictures a dream within a dream cinematically and if it is possible to retrieve the unconscious moment that signals the end of reel one and the activation of reel two, so to speak, what unique unconscious psychology could account for this cinematographic decision?

The topic was first introduced by Sigmund Freud in 1900 and since then has received scant attention (Berman 1985; Silber 1983, etc.). Whether this means that the phenomenon is rare or simply underreported is not clear.

Freud in 1900 insisted that a dream within a dream was a sure sign that something that had actually happened was being disavowed vehemently. "If a particular event is inserted into a dream … by the dream work itself, this implies the most decided confirmation of the reality of the event" (Freud 1990, p. 338). To place a dream within the envelope of another dream suggested that a reality was being hidden with such precision that an astute awakener would raise his eyebrows at the elaborate mechanism of disguise.

In this paper I would like not only to re-examine Freud's thesis but also to address his neglect of the envelope as he focused solely on its contents. In other words, I will argue that a dream within a dream has two dream portions, one seemingly housed in the other, that both portions are part of one elaborate illusion, and that both can be studied profitably.

One assumption of this paper is that a "formal" re-textualization of the unfolding semiotic of a dream must be in response to the emergence in the dream state of affect that cannot be disguised with the "usual" primary processes (condensation, displacement, symbolism) but requires a fundamental relocation of the drama to resolve or at least manage the conflict and keep the dreamer asleep. That is, reels are switched dramatically for urgent dynamic reasons.

The dream within a dream that is scrutinized here occurred in the eighth year of an analysis, a clinical context that allowed the topic to be viewed through the lens of a complex transference neurosis. Genetics, dynamics, transference, and countertransference had been explicated again and again so that termination was now the focus and perhaps one of the main triggers of the dream.

The dreamer is 56 years old, South African (significant in the sense that he often referred to his enslaved soul as a "Mandela," long incarcerated but yearning to be free), an ex-priest, a professor of philosophy, recently married, with one child. The analysis could be portrayed as the deconstruction of a conscience so Jesuitical in its brilliant mixture of menace, mischief, and multiple ambiguities as to be almost unreachable, its mental quicksilver visible, touchable, but hard to pick up or hold onto.

The dream was reported as follows:

I awake at the sound of a car pulling into the driveway of our Connecticut house. It is pitch dark, but a child is being dropped off as if our home were a nursery school. All this seemed natural in a dream experience even though the time, the darkness, would have been highly unusual for such a drop-off in real time. The scene shifts. I am now outside my house but lost, trying to find my bearings. A child on a bicycle guides me home. Then I walk from my house in Connecticut to Greenwich Village, which in my dream geography seems no more than a hundred yards. I am so surprised by the spatial novelty of Connecticut's [being] a stone's throw from Greenwich Village that I wake up, an illusion, as I will discover on actual awakening. In Greenwich Village I walk into a wood-lined office in a townhouse. A bearded man, not unlike the young Freud in the Freud-Fliess era, greets me. I start to tell him

3

the unusual dream I've just had about being lost and how it was a child who guided me home.

When the dreamer awakes he begins to tell his wife the dream immediately and while recounting the dream has a *déjà vu* phenomenon, as if he had told her the dream already. He is aware that the dream-within-a-dream phenomenon of telling the dream to the bearded man in Greenwich Village is what gives the *déjà vu* experience with his wife such an uncanny feeling.

(A dream followed by a *déjà vu* feeling is noteworthy, a point I will address later.)

The associations were genetic, dynamic, free-flowing, and far-ranging. New insights were generated as dream and dream within dream were examined for several weeks. The theme of a lost childhood as well as an actual experience of being lost at age five, had been analyzed from various angles down the years. But the dream-within-a-dream treatment of it seemed to generate new affects, more intense memory. The analysand, whose reading of Freud was deep and well-integrated into his overall philosophical knowledge (a factor that could be a resistance at times but often was a promoter of insight) was not unaware of Freud's contributions to the topic. "One hides in a dream within a dream an actual event," he commented, paraphrasing Freud. "In that case, depending on which of the dreams is within the other, being lost could be the disavowed actuality, or is it 'telling' about it that is the significant reality that is being relegated to dream life, doubly displaced, and captioned as non-real in its dream-within-dream status?" Several questions had been raised that would take time to address. If there was no new "topic" at this stage of analysis, the same could not be said of affect. Memory and history were not files in an unconscious library but sudden revelations of the self in a living mirror that could surprise and astonish no matter how clever the defensive anticipations.

Which part of the dream was within the other? If the totality of the dream is looked upon as one text, the illusion of waking up and telling the dream to a bearded man in Greenwich Village would seem to be the part of the dream that is within the other, larger, earlier part. However, looking at the dream as a total text, one could argue that the first part is being told again in the later dream and is therefore "within" it, making the analysand's question not as "intellectual" as it seemed at first blush. This raises the question as to whether the two dream pieces can be studied in isolation or separately, a task Silber (1983) set himself in his brilliant paper on the topic, no doubt to keep his focus scientific and uncluttered.

Which actuality was being disguised, the experience of being lost or the telling about it? This led to a series of intriguing sessions, but some genetic context must be described to make the narrative intelligible.

Mr. Perdu (a fictitious name for the analysand) had recounted early in his analysis how once as a child in Johannesburg he had been playing with older boys who suddenly went about their own business, forgetting the younger one who'd been entrusted to their care. He imagines that he was five or six in the memory. A kind gentleman on a bicycle rode him home to his house. In later years, whenever this incident was recalled, his mother would rail against the boy to whom she had entrusted her son, taking little responsibility for her own negligence. Mr. P was aware that in the dream "a child on a bicycle who guided him home" was a reversal of the actual roles of child and adult 50 years before the dream. This childhood memory had been analyzed intensely, but the reversal and the elaborate dream work that dream-within-dream implied suggested, as Freud would have argued, that this was the reality whose disavowal in dream-within-dream was in fact a powerful affirmation of its significance.

Mr. P, an only child, had for years insisted that a great closeness had existed between him and his mother—an assertion that memory and dream seemed to challenge. His father's alcoholism and fiscal irresponsibility left the family in dire straits often, until the mother started her own business and essentially became the breadwinner. The father's character was dramatically revealed in a childhood memory: in bed with the father after a bad dream, the child urinated while asleep. The father, startled, reprimanded the child, creating a sense of distance between son and father that was never redressed. Years later in analysis, the adult would comment bitterly: "The warm flow of my intimacy was lost on him." He idealized the mother's resourcefulness and courage and could not remember ever feeling any anger toward her.

The anger he felt toward his father could not be expressed either except in pity and shame. A vicious superego became the heir of these unspeakable hatreds for years, quite egosyntonic with the vicious Catholic god Mr. P had enshrined in the Vatican of his mind throughout his preanalytic existence. But an unconscious Mandela was there too, as mentioned earlier, longing to break the shackles. The shackles, like most psychological shackles, were "mind-forged manacles," as Blake suggested, and the forge had a complex artistry that displayed its symptoms but not the mold, which remained well hidden. Mr. P was aware that the dream within a dream had exposed the mold more than ever and that the revelation should be pounced on and exploited. "There's loss in one piece of the dream and telling about it in the other," he exclaimed. This eureka of insight provoked a re-examination of all the previously stoked genetic embers. The concepts of "loss" and "telling" themes that were sounded often, were about to lend themselves to variations that surprised the analysand with their novelty despite their ancient origins. Loss had been a theme that both antedated and postdated the actual childhood loss that occurred, when his older playmates abandoned him. The oedipal years were characterized by incestuous closeness to a mother who had distanced herself from a negligent husband, seducing her son, figuratively speaking, with confidences and intimacies that belonged more appropriately in the relationship with her husband.

"There's no telling what I was told," the analysand would quip ironically and cynically as he tried to invoke the childhood atmosphere of loneliness and closeness, a paradox that made more and more sense to him as he explored the absence of his father from his life and the undifferentiated presence of his mother. The "loss" of his father had been passively experienced in the sense that Mr. P never questioned his father's self-destructive character or his mother's compliance with it. He never "told" his father off for his chronic neglect, and he never told his mother off for her abandonment of her dialogue with his father and "seduction" of her son. Instead, he assumed that his "loss" was coming to him, something he deserved for secretly hating both of them. The actual incident of loss at age five, traumatic and real, in itself, was also a screen for deeper losses. Religion was "telling" in the ironic sense that the analysand felt he was telling very private intimacies to the wrong people, priests who in hindsight often seemed unworthy of this revelations. Minor childhood symptoms of latency stealing were adjudicated as major crimes in the confession box, a kind of childhood supreme court that would eventually, of course, take up permanent residence in his superego, through processes of introjection and identification. In retrospect he realized that he hated his mother for supporting a primitive institution that exploited a child's guilt rather than explaining it and exploring it empathically, as analysis would do many years later. "I should have told the priest off. Instead, I swallowed my guts and became a priest myself, identification with the aggressor and victim all at once I suppose." The bitterness of this reconstruction was palpable as insight savored anew the old love, the old hatred, the relentless conflict.

That his life was about being lost and telling people about it had become more central in the analysis than ever before, thanks to the double vision of the dream and the insight it afforded about the meaning of loss and the meaning of communication (telling) and how both could be corrupted by a defensive psychology that would attempt to keep them apart. "It will be important for me to tell you how much I hate you as termination reprises this sense of loss for yet another time," the analysand said, stepping into the reality of the analytic journey's end with very genuine affect.

The many meanings of the dream-within-dream psychology were uncovered in this rich free-associative process. Telling intimacies to parent, priest, analyst seemed to be one psychological seed of the dream process; loss as experience, loss as unconscious punishment or fear, the other.

The dream thoughts beneath the manifest content of both segments of the dream sequence could be summarized as follows:

The child "delivered" to the house at an "odd" hour is the wish to have a child in the primal scene. The primal crime of the first part of the dream is punished by loss of bearings, loss of home. This stirs up the reality of the actual traumatic loss in childhood, which is reversed in the representation of "a child guided me home." This reversal seems not adequate to the task; "reel switching" becomes necessary. In the "new" dream portion, after the illusion of awakening there is confession to a bearded man who represents father and analyst (neither one bearded in reality). "Beard" represents undoing of the wish to castrate father and analyst for "forcing" him to confess, for not having a baby with him, for not allowing him to be a permanent analytic baby, for forcing him out as termination approaches. The distance between Connecticut ("connect" as opposite to the "disconnection" of loss) and Greenwich Village is "destroyed," time space altered magically in the new "Greenwich Mean Time" of unconscious timelessness.

This summary does not address the central question of this paper even though it is an essential preamble. The analysand's intellectual doggedness about the dream-within-a-dream mechanism was the engine that generated more and more free-associative information about what he playfully referred to as this "unconscious curiosity." The possibility of reaching a compromise between the wish to tell the dream to someone and the wish to stay asleep was entertained as one potential motivation, but there were deeper currents also, he felt sure.

Mr. P was puzzled that the reality of being lost as a child, which had received much scrutiny in the analysis, could still show up in a dream within a dream, as if to insist that it still needed to be disavowed intensely! We had reconstructed it pretty well. Which stone had been left unturned? As Mr. P pursued this issue associatively, overwhelming "new" affects appeared genetically and transferentially. Deep-seated anger toward mother emerged. How could she have entrusted a five-year-old to careless older boys? What did that reveal about the whole ramshackle structure of early care he must have received from a harried young mother starting her own business on the ruins of her husband's psychological and fiscal collapse? Who was this makeshift father; what made him tick? This genetic current of intense affect could turn transferential from hour to hour. What kind of an analyst could have reconstructed so intellectually, leaving the deepest affects untouched? Was the analyst lost in some dream within a dream of his own to have overlooked the most significant meanings? This analytic volatility, genetic and transferential all at once, led to the revelation that the reality of childhood loss had not been fully analyzed, if it ever could be. It was clear that affect would always remain. Sorrow, pain, anger, memory could be understood in analysis but not eliminated, not exorcised. The confessional offered absolution, the wipe-out of sin. The couch could offer only understanding, the sober dignity of truth rather than the appeal of illusion!

Communication itself was corrupted in childhood, be believed, when "telling" to a priest became mandatory. Even when he was no longer a priest, the inquisitional dialogue continued within, in the internal confessional. Much of the analytic work in the transference neurosis was an attempt to rehabilitate communication itself, to rescue it from its inquisitional origins. By putting trauma in one dream and "telling" in a dream within it, the analysand was declaring that "telling" was as great a trauma as trauma itself, and that the two should not be confused. If he had been able to "tell" his mother off for entrusting him carelessly to the older boys, the original trauma might not have retained its "actual" significance or its symbolic significance as a screen for all the other "tellings" that had been left unsaid. Considering the first part of the dream as the dream within the larger dream (the dream in its totality), the analysand argued that the child guiding him home could be viewed as a fulfillment of the wish that the older boy had not betrayed him or, better still, that he had been able to tell the boy off and demand that the boy not betray him but guide him home. The capacity to talk straight to one's peers in childhood (or adulthood, for that matter) is a measure of how "straight" one felt one could be in the dialogue with father or mother. Developmental achievement cannot be sustained without some early object constancy. If the breast is the first curriculum, baby talk is the first dialogue. Essentially telling and loving go hand in hand unless the system breaks down for defensive reasons.

If one undoes the division between the two dream parts and treats the text as a seamless document, one reading of the text could be articulated as follows: "I want a baby delivered to me in darkness, a primal-scene reversal in which I am not excluded. For this, the punishment is loss of the object or loss of the love of the object" (castration fear disavowed perhaps as "regressive" object loss screens the more oedipal punish-ment). "'A child guided me home' redresses this. Finally, the wish to tell all to a bearded man represents the undoing of the father's castration and a man-to-man dialogue between son and parent in which aggression and sexuality need not be denied in the new space analysis has cleared for straight talk."

If that was the seamless vision of the dream, why was the illusion of dream within dream necessary at all? To all the defensive reasons alluded to earlier, the analysand added that a dream within a dream is like one dream spawning another. The wish to have the oedipal baby with the analyst, with the mother, with the father, could be represented through the formal disguise of one dream giving birth to another, one dream invaginated in the other in an act of oneiric copulation. One dream was the dream child of the other, so to speak. When the analysis ended, the patient remarked with characteristic irony, "There's no telling what the future holds." While this was obviously true, it seemed clear that the future would hold a more enlightened vision of the past and that a dream within a dream could claim some of the credit for it.

Discussion

The concept of a dream within a dream, first introduced by Freud in 1900, usually serves as the starting point for all subsequent inquiry. While Freud is very assertive as to the meaning of the phenomenon, the clinical evidence that would justify such theoretical certitude is not cited. Was Freud's clinical specimen too personal perhaps, too self-revealing? It is unlikely that the question can ever be answered. But we can assume that Freud had an actual dream-within-a-dream experience in mind when he stated, "To include something in a 'dream within a dream' is thus equivalent to wishing that the thing described as a dream had never happened... . If a particular event is inserted into a dream ... by the dream work itself, this implies the most decided confirmation of the reality of the event—the strongest *affirmation* of it" (Freud 1990, p. 338). This sounds like dogma rather than science unless the actual clinical evidence is produced so that the reasoning behind it can be assessed.

Let us try to imagine the specimen dream within a dream Freud was commenting on: A dream is unfolding. An infantile wish is struggling to represent itself in the distorted disguised manner that Freud himself was the first to elucidate so ingeniously. Is Freud suggesting that if this "usual" process of disguised wish fulfillment stirs up an actual traumatic memory, stumbles on an actual piece of historic truth, the alarmed dreamer, close to nightmare, will change the subject drastically and spin a new dream in which to disavow the "reality" that had threatened to destroy the precarious dream structure and ruin a good night's sleep? In a sense the dream-within-a-dream strategy wards off an impending nightmare by switching reels, to invoke the cinematographic metaphor once again. All defense could be viewed as an unconscious strategic change of subject, usually a lot more subtle than stopping a dream in its tracks and starting a new one. Can we assume that the unconscious engine that drives all defensive strategy can lose its subtlety, regressively perhaps, in an emergency such as the verge of nightmare in a dream state would represent? Are there any developmental prototypes of this drastic, primitive, clumsy kind of deployment of defense? A child at play offers the most graphic depiction of sudden subject changing. A child depicting oedipal subject matter in triadic representations of horse, lion, and tiger in conflict at a moment of extreme anxiety may toss horse, lion, and tiger aside and start a new play schema involving sheep, cow, and donkey! To the child analyst observer this may seem a lot more obviously defensive that it appears to the child. What seems crude to the adult may seem subtle to the child at play. Similarly, in the dream state, reel-switching that sets the dream-within-dream strategy in motion may seem like a subtle escape clause to the dreamer even if it appears crude or obvious to the sophisticated Freudian awakener.

Are there other prototypes of the dream-within-dream experience that the unconscious dream cinematographer can exploit as he rummages through the prop rooms of the past? Can one assume that the dream stagehands are resourceful and can "use" any prior experience of the dreamer however they like in the service of disguise? Just as the unconscious can be aware of somatic illness sooner than the consciousness of the patient, announcing illness in dream life before the diagnosis has been arrived at, can we assume that the unconscious, once it has "experienced" a sense of deperson-alization, for instance, can subsequently "use" it in dream life as an "out of body" feeling or an "out of dream" feeling such as a dream within a dream would entail? I am suggesting that once there has been a feeling of the uncanny in waking life, what's to stop dream life from recycling it unconsciously and reprising it in dream life as a dream within a dream? Surely it is this kind of uncanny recycling that the poet tries to cap-ture when he says, "La vida es sueño" (Calderón de la Barca 1636) or "our little life is rounded with a sleep" (Shakespeare 1611, Act 4 Scene 10). If this implies an even greater continu-ity between dream life and waking life than is usually thought of, a reciprocal cross-fertilization of one by the other, it may also highlight a cultural mistrust of the oneiric in Occidental circles, Oriental culture being far less discriminating when it comes to distinguishing dream life from waking life, as the title of Wendy Doniger O'Flaherty's (1984), astute study, "Dreams, Illusions and Other Realities," suggests.

To return to Freud's pronouncement that material in a dream within a dream is absolute evidence of a reality that is being disavowed: unless a dynamic sequence of dream events is invoked that leads to the eruption onto the dream stage of an alarming piece of reality, which then must be dealt with drastically by banishment into a new dream space altogether, it is difficult to know how to make sense of Freud's categorical assertion. Without the dynamic as-sociative trail of oneiric events that lead to the eruption of the unwanted reality into the dream and its subsequent expulsion into the illusion of the adjoining dream, we would have to take Freud's word for it without any proof, an exer-cise in blind faith that the founder of psychoanalysis would not endorse even when his own scientific data are under scrutiny. In this instance we need the clinical existence of Freud's dream-within-dream data before we can pass judg-ment on the merit of the theory. It is for this reason that I have dared to imagine the clinical legs Freud's theory stands on.

When it comes to Mr. Perdu, we do have the clinical legs to guide us toward the theory that informs the dream-within-a-dream strategy. I began this paper by suggesting that the moment that signals the end of a sense of seamless dreaming and the start of the illusion of another dream sequence must be an indication of intense, unique, unconscious psychology. What can be inferred from Mr. Perdu's analysis and the occurrence of the dream within a dream?

Following Freud's line of reasoning, can it be assumed that the memory of a most painful piece of reality began to emerge and had to be disavowed with frantic dispatch and relocated in a new setting, given that the old setting of the original dream was massively endangered by its emerging traumatic presence? The moment of "reel switching" would seem to have occurred when the dreamer was lost and a child on a bicycle was guiding him home. By switching reels at this moment and seeming to begin a new dream, the content of the first reel is being designated as "a dream within a dream," the better to disavow the reality that had appeared too blatantly, too undisguisedly, in the dream. A piece of historic truth had threatened to challenge the soothing, sleep-enhancing narrative truth of the dream and needed to be relegated to the status of "not real" by the dream-within-dream strategy as if to insist that "it's only a dream" needed the added reinforcement "it's only a dream within a dream. How could I ever have mistaken it for reality?" Freud does not comment on the content of the subsequent dream—"the usurper dream," so to speak—as if its meaning were insignificant, unimportant. This is a curious piece of neglect since we can be almost certain that reel two has some deeply significant relationship to reel one, no matter how fundamental the disguise might appear. Mr. Perdu goes so far as to question which piece of dream is within the other. While this Jesuitical intellectuality could be treated as characterological and is quite characteristic of his defensive maneuvers, the question nevertheless contains an insight to which he associated diligently and profitably. Mr. Perdu clearly recognized the urgency in reel one that signaled the unconscious cinematographer to switch reels, but he doubted that the content of reel two was any less significant than that of reel one, even it its *raison d'être* was indeed to displace and disguise "the reality" that reel one could not tolerate. Mr. Perdu even suggested that the content of reel two was prefigured in reel one, the terror of one re-stated in the other rather than eliminated entirely. At the moment of unconscious terror in reel one, when the panic of a lost child emerged, did the reality of the father's utter absence from Mr. Perdu's life, coupled with an intense yearning for contact with him, emerge also with such painful affect that the father (young, bearded man) and the dialogue with him had to be isolated in its own new dream surroundings, far removed from the dream dynamics that had gotten it started in the first place?

Mr. Perdu had told his young, bearded father his dreams, placed all his faith in him, even offered him the warm sexual intimacy of nocturnal enuresis, only to be rejected, abandoned, lost. This "reality," played out in confessionals, in becoming a church "father" (priest), in analysis itself, would need to be jettisoned from waking life (even from "typical" dream life), at home only in the peculiar illusion of a usurping dream portion of a dream within a dream until the transference neurosis could make it fully acceptable in the dialogue with the analyst. What was not "told" to the father and was "told" only in confessionals with a bitter ambivalence would have to be told to an analyst who could not only tolerate intense hatred and love but cherish the act of "listening" that would engage the act of "telling," no matter how conflicted the dialogue would become in the new therapeutic setting.

This discussion of the dream-within-a-dream process is different from Freud's (1900), Berman's (1985) and Silber's (1983) in the emphasis it places on both portions of the dream and the dynamic links between them. While Berman, comparing the dream-within-dream process to the primal scene, refers to the inner dream and the outer dream, the dynamic link between dream within dream and "usurper" dream is not spelt out. Silber, as mentioned earlier, tries to focus only on the dream-within-dream segment of his example, and Freud, as cited, did not give details of the dream within a dream, nor did he mention or place any emphasis at all on the subsequent dream (what I've been calling the usurper dream). By drawing attention to the dynamic linkage between the two portions of the dream sequence I believe that the multiple determinants of both are enriched and highlighted.

I have also suggested an analogy between the bifurcated form of the dream-within-dream strategy and other conceivable prototypes, such as childhood play, splitting and altered states of consciousness such as fugues and depersonalizations. What significance can be attached to the *déjà vu* feeling the awakener experienced when recounting the dream to his wife? This does suggest that the act of telling the dream to the bearded man and subsequently to the wife are "uncannily" related to the conflicted communications with father, mother, and priest, from an earlier era, conflicted childhood communications, which become repressed and unconscious, always residing "within" adult consciousness, not too dissimilar perhaps from the experience of dream within dream itself. In that sense, the post-dream déjà vu feeling is a reprise of the dream-within-dream experience, highlighting it, accentuating its meaning, haunting the awakener with a mysterious revenant of dream-lore.

References

Berman, L. (1985). Primal scene significance of a dream within a dream, *Int. J. Psycho-Anal.*, 66:75–76.

Blake, W. (1794). "London" from *Song of Experience.* Norton Anthology of Poetry. 3rd Edition, London. New York: W. W. Norton & Company, 1983.

Calderón de la Barca, P. (1636). *La vida es sueño.* Denver: University Press of Colorado. 2004.

Freud, S. (1900). The interpretation of dreams. *S.E.* 4.

O'Flaherty, W. D. (1984). *Dreams, Illusion and Other Realities.* Chicago: Univ. Chicago Press.

Silber, A. (1983). A significant dream within a dream. *J. Amer. Psychoanal. Assn.* 31:899–915.

Shakespeare, W. (1564–1616).*The Tempest.* Cambridge: Harvard Univ. Press, 1958.

Dreams and Other Ways

William Fried

My invitation to contribute this article asked that I comment on a paper about a dream within a dream by Eugene Mahon. After reading Mahon's (2002) paper several times, I decided to forego an attempt at a detailed critique in favor of using it as a point of departure for a meditation on the theme of this volume: whether dreams may still be regarded as the Royal Road to the unconscious. That Mahon, himself, may accept this proposition is suggested first, by the meticulous attention he pays to dreams in this and other papers, by the seriousness with which he takes the task of disproving Freud's (1900) contention that "If a particular event is inserted into a dream ... by the dream work itself, this implies the most decided confirmation of the reality of the event," and by his disclosing that he and his patient spent several weeks analyzing the dream in question. Thus, although he does not state, explicitly, that he believes the dream is uniquely privileged, as Freud did, his approach and general attitude to dream analysis is far from being at odds with such an assumption.

As a practicing analyst who is deeply interested in dreams and other products of the imagination, I inevitably compared my own beliefs and approaches to dreams with those of Mahon throughout each of my several readings of his paper. Among the initial results of this comparison was the impression that Mahon's work with dreams was a great deal more "classical" than mine. That is, he seems, at least tacitly, to accept and use Freud's methods of dream interpretation as a template to be followed faithfully except, as in the single instance of the dream within a dream, where he feels justified in challenging the Master. Further, the phrasing and organization of his challenge has the same air of respect as theologians' approaches to scripture.

If pressed to subscribe to a particular theoretical orientation, I would probably first express earnest objections to the question on the grounds of its resemblance to an item on a forced choice test that allows for no deviation from the psychometrist's phrasing. Next, I would try to clarify that the question doesn't discriminate among the theoretical, clinical, technical, and aesthetic components of various psychoanalytic tributaries, each of which, and aspects of which, may be preferred to others. For the purposes of this paper, however, I am content to identify myself as fundamentally Freudian, since that will give me license to specify how, despite our common ancestry, Mahon and I diverge.

To begin with, as I've already hinted, were I to meet a Freud who'd survived into the 21st Century, I fancy I would be respectful but not reverent. I would expect him to have known about the many changes in psychoanalytic thought since he began to invent it, and to have evaluated and revealed his opinions of them, as was his wont throughout his career. Some, he would anatomize, scrutinize their parts, and subject them to the kinds of ingenious refutation that comprise the subjects of many of his writings. But, for the ones that he felt could be woven into his complex fabric, he might immediately find a place or, initially rejecting them, incorporate them later on. As an imaginary example, consider what he would have done with the findings of Aserinsky, Kleitman (1953), Dement (1957), et al., and their successors, regarding conjugate rapid eye movements, and the absence of muscle tone everywhere in the body save the eyes and genitals during REM periods. Coincidentally, I would think it highly probable that these research data might have given Freud decisive support in pronouncing the dream to be the royal road. In that case, however, he would be thinking theoretically. Whether he'd then find a way of integrating this new knowledge into his theory of therapy or technique, is a different matter.

An analyst who uses *The Interpretation of Dreams* (Freud, 1900) as a manual would, of necessity, have to devote a great deal of time to attend to the patient's narration, elicit associations to every aspect of the content, study the day residue, deal with the secondary elaboration, arrive at an interpretation, etc. Mahon's exposition strongly suggests that he and his patient conducted their treatment of the dream, if not in absolute adherence to Freud's model, at least in a close simulacrum. Since the analysis seems to have consisted of four or five sessions per week, this regime is certainly plausible. What is more questionable, however, is the absence, in Mahon's report, of moments or events that might have given him pause for the kind of puzzlement or self doubt that occurs in the experience of any analyst, indeed, of any clinician, from time to time.

It is my impression that Mahon and his patient both have a scholar's familiarity with Freud's oeuvre. In addition, both seem richly erudite, and extraordinarily intellectualized. For better or worse, then, these traits lend to their analytic discourse an uncommon degree of the ideational as opposed to, or as a dilution of, a more spontaneously expressive dialogue. To the degree that my observations are accurate in this respect, there seems to have been an implicit agreement between the two men that their mutual project would encompass as many of the features of a "classical" analysis, along with the mandatory and equally "classical," attention to dreams, as possible.

It seems to me that this classicism carried an array of preconceptions that informed the conduct of the analyst, and the analysand. As with all preconceptions, these appeared to have been tacitly accepted and, hence, to remain un-interrogated. For example, the author's insistence on regarding clinical psychoanalysis as a "science" rather than a hermeneutic procedure would require that we believe his interpretations to be the definitive ones or the only ones permissible. In parallel fashion, he would assert that we accept only the patient's material on which he based his interpretations, and reject or ignore the rest. Further, we would be obliged to endorse the propositions that every dream is instigated by an infantile wish, and that there exists a set of dream symbols that invariably encode specific ideas and not others.

If these characterizations of Mahon's approach in the sample contained in this paper are accurate, I believe he would reply "yes" to the question of whether dreams are still the royal road. There would be no reason to doubt that his (and his patient's) attitude to Freud's thought, even his deferential manner in challenging it, reflect a kind of sanctification.

My own take on the eponymous question is that any type of clinical material as well as the armamentarium of techniques that may be applied to it may come to qualify as the royal road depending on its function at a given time and context of the analysis. That is, every clinical encounter contains a particular clue that, when it is discovered, renders the remaining material intelligible. The clue can as well be a locution of the patient's, an enactment, a silence, an affective expression, a gesture or posture, as it might be a dream. And I would add, taking a leaf from Freud's book, that just as a forbidden or disturbing thought may be disguised as apparently the least significant element of a dream, it may also seek refuge and disguise outside of a dream in some other seemingly trivial piece of behavior.

Early in my career, under the influence of respected teachers and supervisors, my interventions tended to be removed by varying degrees from my patients' immediate experiences. My rationale was that they needed to grasp the dynamics underlying their behavior. Some of my patients seemed receptive to this, but many did not. I was often vacillating between the wish to emulate my mentors and the realization that I was not reaching most of my patients. Here, the question of what constitutes a "correct" interpretation, and its corollary, by what criteria do we arrive at it, are paramount. For it may be posited that the most "correct" interpretation is that which reaches deepest into the causality of a behavior, i.e., gets to the metapsychological root of it. And who could argue that such an assertion lacks merit. The sole objection to it is that in the vast majority of clinical situations it is likely to have little therapeutic value: worse, it is almost certain to be taken as evidence of the analyst's failure to understand the patient and accordingly will become a locus of resistance if not a buttress for intellectual defenses.

One of my patients began a recent session by describing a dream in which he met a co-worker who'd died a few years ago. They'd been friends for a long time, but had a falling out a year or two before the man's death. It had been precipitated by the co-worker's outrage at my patient's failure to support him for a promotion that my patient felt was unmerited. In the dream, they greeted each other effusively with warm handshakes that signaled that their differences had been resolved and their friendship restored. He emphasized how happy this made him feel.

My patient said that he did not know what to make of the dream but his wife, to whom he told it, thought it applied to another friendship of his, this with a man to whom he'd been very close over a period of decades but who, recently seemed to take distance from him. He thought this plausible but not especially enlightening, and moved on to other subjects that he wanted to discuss. Recently retired, he described steps to take up a new hobby and resign from a part-time teaching position.

The relevant background of this vignette is that the patient has been depressed about the absence of direction and meaning in his life after retirement. He is also convinced that he has lost his conversational fluency, becoming tongue-tied at social gatherings, and unable to access the word he wishes to use in routine speech. He has been evaluated for cognitive and memory deficits with no evidence for either being found. His depression is also related to erectile dysfunction and a generalized anhedonia that is often enough broken through by pleasant and pleasurable experiences from which, predictably, he soon returns to his baseline dejection. His wife and children are very supportive and devoted to him and he has a wide circle of friends with whom he engages regularly despite regarding himself as socially inept.

Referring to the dream in the session that followed, he again commented on how happy he was to be reconciled with his former friend. He also mentioned his wife's idea that the friend in the dream was a proxy for the one who has currently cooled towards him. I asked him why he would have to substitute for the living friend, a dead one. He was unable to explain this but then spoke of his joy in seeing the dead friend alive. This led him to understand that he would feel a comparable joy if he were able to breathe life into a relationship that he was afraid had become moribund and, even more cogently, to breathe life back into himself.

There would have been an ample basis for asking the patient to associate to all the elements of the dream, and trace this material to early familial origins. Indeed, this patient would have welcomed such a procedure and participated in it with enthusiasm. What I did, instead, was to wait and see what would emerge. I have long accepted the hypothesis that any of the material in a session where a dream has been presented may be associations to the dream, whether or not it is so labelled, and whether or not it has been elicited by explicit work on the dream. Often this is borne out; sometimes not. My point is that using a self-conscious method such as the one Freud demonstrated in *The Interpretation of Dreams*, one that seems to have been emulated to a considerable degree by Mahon and his patient, might stultify and render formulaic any interpretation that would result.

Further, I should confess that often my approach to dreams does not include any attempt at interpretation or discovering a discursive meaning. At other times, after asking the patient what she makes of a dream, I will accept her inclination either to continue to engage with it or to let it alone, but I will not stop listening for associations in whatever came before or after the dream, even sessions later, as in my example. My reason is the belief that rich and unforeseen matter tends to emerge unbidden when spontaneity is optimal.

But I have another basis for often refraining from trying to interpret or decipher the dream: it is that I am aware of a wish (the patient's and mine) that the dream stand alone, uninterpreted, having retained its distinctly dream's reality and thereby embodying a special value. I don't want to translate it into expository prose and then throw it away, emptied of its contents. I am less interested in analyzing dreams than in rescuing them from the processes of dilution, fading, disillusionment, and utility, which would deprive them of their unique difference from ordinary experience. Moreover, I believe that this way of receiving a dream has distinct therapeutic virtue. I am asserting that there is at least as much value in the pleasures of dreams and dreaming as in their interpretation. And further, that our patients can benefit as much from the one as from the other. This suggests that there is an entire realm of the therapeutic that has remained consciously unexplored although its effects have doubtlessly been applied and felt subversively.

I suspect that all the psychoanalysts who take a special interest in dreams, fantasies, movies, plays, novels, poems, and other works of the imagination are similarly drawn to their magical qualities, their dialectical function as an antidote to reality, and that they use the conceit of interpretation as the price of admission to a domain whose pleasures might otherwise be deemed forbidden.

We can conceive of many but not all dreams as the patients' poetry, imaginative entities that are brought to the analyst with the hope, implicit or explicit, that she will appreciate their special qualities and help the patient to appreciate them. This can occur through interpretation, but more because the act of interpretation demonstrates the analyst's riveted attention than the unraveling of the content. One essential reason that every patient has sought analysis is that she has repeatedly lost the attention of those in her life to whom she most wanted to communicate the things that she most needed them to know. She could not share these with anyone else and, so, in desperation, she has taken the risk of engaging with this attentive stranger, this psychoanalyst.

Just as filmmakers create narratives for audiences, the analysand collaborates with her analyst to create a narrative that differs from the one she was given early in her life. That narrative has been spoken and enacted in myriad ways. She is the protagonist of her own play. One of the motives for her seeking psychotherapy is that she has been playacting, that is, enacting a role in her play. Among the goals she is seeking are to stop playacting and enacting, and to start playing and acting. To act, in this context, means to depart from the received script, to improvise, to do things differently. To play means to live, for as long as may be necessary, in imaginative circumstances where variability of all kinds is possible. I am proposing that the function of appreciation, in contrast to interpretation, contributes most to the creation of these imaginative circumstances. It entails the willing suspension of disbelief and what Marianne Moore described as "imaginary gardens with real toads in them," a wonderful metaphor of transference.

Because a dream may be felt as qualitatively different from other material and be brought to the analyst as a gift or offering, immediate interpretive measures, including the deliberate elicitation of associations, may be felt as a rejection by the patient, and a premature divestment of enchantment from the dream. I am here proposing nothing less than that one essential function of psychoanalysis is to help the patient to an acceptance and valuation of this domain of experience as a central component of one's inner life. In this connection, I would remind the reader of Winnicott's idea that the infant's attachment to transitional objects and related phenomena metamorphoses to an interest in all the realms of culture, as she develops towards adulthood. Thus, alongside the analytic work of helping the patient to achieve a firmer and more ego-syntonic grasp of reality, and balancing it, is the focus on enlarging and refining the capacity for play in all its forms. To quote Winnicott (1953):

> This intermediate area of experience, unchallenged in respect of its belonging to inner or external (shared) reality, constitutes the greater part of the infant's experience and throughout life is retained in the intense experiencing that belongs to the arts and to religion and to imaginative living, and to creative scientific work.

The literary critic, Susan Sontag (1990), devoted an entire book to this, and related propositions. It is titled *Against Interpretation*, and I interpolate the following excerpt from one of its essays, "On Style," in support of my argument and to credit her as a source of my thinking.

> I am not saying that a work of art creates a world which is entirely self-referring. Of course, works of art (with the exception of music) refer to the real world—to our knowledge, to our experience, to our values. They present information and evaluations. But their distinctive

feature is that they give rise not to conceptual knowledge (which is the distinctive feature of discursive or scientific knowledge—e.g., philosophy, sociology, psychology, history) but to something like an excitation, a phenomenon of commitment, judgment in a state of thralldom or captivation. Which to say that the knowledge we gain through art is an experience of the form or style of knowing something, rather than a knowledge of something (like a fact or a moral judgment) in itself.

This explains the preeminence of the value of expressiveness in works of art; and how the value of expressiveness—that is, of style—rightly takes precedence over content (when content is, falsely, isolated from style). The satisfactions of Paradise Lost for us do not lie in its views on God and man, but in the superior kinds of energy, vitality, and expressiveness which are incarnated in the poem.

Hence, too, the peculiar dependence of works of art, however expressive, upon the cooperation of the person having the experience, for one may see what is "said" but remain unmoved, either through dullness or distraction. Art is seduction, not rape. A work of art proposes a type of experience designed to manifest the quality of imperiousness. But art cannot seduce without the complicity of the experiencing subject.

Returning, now, to the consideration of whether Freud's positing the dream as the royal road to the unconscious remains valid, I fear my contribution to be equivocal. For, if my assertion that the aesthetic approach to dreams is as important as the analytic is accepted, a necessary consequence would be that the royal road is more a function of the analyst's receptive attitude than of the inherent quality of the material that is shared. The caveat, however, is that dreams, unlike many other classes of material, come wrapped in an aura of wonder, of alternate reality, arcane consciousness. They are, therefore, repositories and representatives of the unknown, and at the same time of psychic regions to which the patient imputes unique significance.

Because a similar aura may envelop other classes of material, it cannot be said that dreams are the only royal road, but they are perhaps the most frequently trod one. It may be instructive, here, to use another literary example to illustrate the process by which an object that, on the face of it, is at the opposite pole from dreams in its ordinariness, may nonetheless attain an equally magical aspect. The passage is the well-known exposition of James Joyce's (1963) concept of epiphany. The speaker is the narrator of the novel titled *Stephen Hero,* from which much of the material for his better known *Portrait of the Artist as a Young Man* was drawn.

–By an epiphany he meant a sudden spiritual manifestation, whether in the vulgarity of speech, or of gesture, or in a memorable phase of the mind itself. He believed that it was for the man of letters to record these epiphanies with extreme care, seeing that they themselves are the most delicate and evanescent of moments. He told Cranly that the clock of the Ballast Office was capable of an epiphany. Cranly questioned the inscrutable dial of the Ballast Office with his no less inscrutable countenance:

–Yes, said Stephen. I will pass it time *after* time, allude to it, refer to it, catch a glimpse of it. It is only an item in the catalogue of Dublin's street furniture. Then all at once I see it and I know at once what it is: epiphany.

–What?

–Imagine my glimpses at that clock as the gropings of a spiritual eye which seeks to adjust its vision to an exact focus. The moment the focus is reached the object is epiphanised. It is just in this epiphany that I find the third, the supreme quality of beauty.

It is by the process of epiphany that the ordinary is rendered extraordinary. How, exactly, an epiphany occurs may not be specifiable but what is clear is that the probability of its occurrence is enhanced by the intensity of attention given to the source of the experience that becomes epiphanised, in our case, the patient. Accordingly, any event that occurs in an analysis, no matter its intrinsic qualities, may acquire the radiance of an epiphany. This view may gain confirmation from the many instances in which a patient, when asked to recall a particularly mutative moment in her analysis, will frequently cite something that the analyst could never have predicted. I therefore submit that there is more than one, and probably many royal roads of which dreams may be the most often cited but perhaps not the most representative.

References

Aserinsky, E. & Kleitman, N. (1953). Regularly occurring periods of eye motility, and concomitant phenomena, during sleep. *Science*, Sept. 4; 118 (3062): 273–4.

Dement, W. & Kleitman, E. (1957). The relation of eye movements during sleep to dream activity: an objective method for the study of dreaming. *J. Exp. Psychol.* 53 (5): 339–346.

Freud, Sigmund. (1900). The Interpretation of Dreams. *S.E.* 4.

Joyce, J. (1963). *Stephen Hero*. New York, New Directions Publishing.

Mahon, E. (2002). Dreams within dreams. *Psychoanal. Study Child*, (57): 118–130.

Sontag, S. (1990). "On Style," in *Against Interpretation*. New York, Anchor Books. Palatine, IL.

Winnicott, D.W. (1953): Transitional objects and transitional phenomena. *I. J. Psychoanal.* 34: 89–97.

Dreams and Dreaming

Arlene Kramer Richards

Abstract

This paper documents the relationship between Freud's dream theory and that of an ancient interpreter of dreams cited several times by Freud: Artemidorus of Daldis. It shows how the method of interpretation of using each scene in a dream, finding associations and symbolism in each, and taking into account the context of the dreamer's life situation that is used by both. It also shows how Freud differed from Artemidorus by investigating the past to find the meaning of the dream while Artemidorus was employed to predict the future. It contends that Freud's interest in the past was directed towards understanding the present and, in particular, to the dream wish. As the wish was a wish for future gratification, Freud's dream interpretation is seen as a more complete, more scientific, more sophisticated version of what Artemidorus did. A theoretical note at the end of the paper attempts to integrate Freud's theory of dreams with modern clinical practice of psychoanalysis.

As a housewife, mother, and part-time college teacher in Topeka, Kansas in the late 1950s, I met Howard Shevrin at a party. He was recruiting for an experiment he was running with a colleague. They were investigating subliminal perception in using as a model an investigation by Potzl. I volunteered. Shown two slides so quickly that I did not register the pictures, I was told to go home and report back the next day to talk about my dreams of that night. I told a story about my how my brother, when he was a tiny boy, used to love to go naked in the woods in New Hampshire where we had a tiny house like a hut out in the woods near a tiny town called Bethlehem. I remember being embarrassed as I told the dream, which felt somehow inauthentic, especially because everything was so tiny.

Later Howie showed me the rebus I had seen but not registered the day before. One was of a man's shirt with collar and tie. The other was a leg, bent at the knee. Tie+knee=tiny. Years later I was a psychologist becoming a psychoanalyst and reading Freud's *Interpretation of Dreams* when I came across this footnote:

> "An important contribution to the part played by recent material in the construction of dreams has been made by Potzl (1917) in a paper which carries a wealth of implications"(Loc.15987).

The footnote explains the same experimental method to which I had been subjected. It stirred my own interest in dreams. A few months ago, I came across a book review that critiqued a new translation of the *Interpretation of Dreams of Appolidorus* and a book describing the place of this book in modern scholarship. The review mentioned that Freud had referred to this book in his *Interpretation of Dreams*. I bought both online within minutes and decided to investigate the influence of Appolidorus on Freud. This paper is an homage to Howie for his work on dreams.

A Chinese Dreamer

Asked why he wrote of blood and violence in his early stories, the Chinese author Wu Hua (2001), responded that:

"It is your experience while growing up, I believe, that shapes the direction of your life. A basic image of the world is planted deep in your mind, and then, like a document in a copy machine, it keeps being reprinted again and again throughout your formative years. Once you reach adulthood, whether you are successful or not, whatever you accomplish can only partially revise that basic image, it will never be entirely transformed" (p. 88).

He went on to say that his father was a surgeon and performed body operations that he saw during his childhood. His school years coincided with the Cultural Revolution; his experience then was full of denunciations, public trials, and subsequent trips to the beach for bloody executions. As an adult he dreamt bloody nightmares. He wrote bloody stories by day and had more nightmares. The cycle was broken when he had a nightmare in which he himself was executed as a murderer. The dream ended with his objecting "Hell, we're not at the beach yet." It was only after that that he recalled the bloody scenes of his childhood and was able to stop dreaming of them and writing of violence with bloody consequences. Yu Hua's reaction to this dream was different from his reaction to all the previous nightmares. The earlier nightmares had fueled his bloody stories. But this dream stopped both the nightmares and the bloody stories.

What was different this time? Could it have been his awareness that all the terrible dreams were about seeing other people die, but in this dream he confronted a fear that he himself could be executed like the people he had witnessed being executed on the beach? Or was it that he spoke up in this last dream and objected to the execution? Did he absolve himself of the guilt of not objecting when others were executed? Or even of guilt at enjoying the dramas? Or was he able to retrieve what he had repressed, retrieve the memories of seeing these horrible scenes, recalling them, and thus laying them to rest? Wu Hua himself believed it was the latter.

If we believe that it was facing the fear that he himself could be executed, we could see the last dream as undoing the displacement of this fear onto others. If it was the objection to being executed, we could see the dream as marking his gaining enough ego strength to defend himself from a death of the mind. If we think that he felt helplessness at seeing the executions, his shame at not being able to stop what was going on was relieved when he dreamt of objecting to the persecution and execution of the victims of this violence. If we thought that he could undo the repression of these early scenes by experiencing the trauma of seeing them, we would be dealing with the return of the repressed. The critic who had first noticed and written to him about the violence of his early stories and the abrupt change in his subject matter was witness to his traumatic past. But so were his earliest readers. In creating the stories, he was writing for the witnesses. We could see this as an unburdening, a sharing, a catharsis. And maybe that was enough to allow him the final dream, the final objection, and the final relief from guilt, shame, and fear.

Understanding Dreams

The great champion and promoter of dream interpretation in modern times was Sigmund Freud. How did he come to believe that dreams are the royal road to the unconscious? And what led him to believe that the unconscious was what drives human behavior? And what had this to do with fate?

One of Freud's great influences was a Greek necromancer, Artemidorus of Daldis who lived in Asia minor in the late second century C.E. His book, *Oneirocritica* (2020 edition), was intended as a handbook for his son to convey all the knowledge and skill the father had accumulated through his career as a dream interpreter who could predict the future from a person's dreams.

He goes about this by dividing dreams into five categories.

The first book is about the human body; the second is about the world outside the body including culture, nature, and religion. The last three books add commentary on miscellaneous themes and objects in dreams.

In this way Artemidorus focused on what psychoanalysis has consistently investigated: the influence of the body and the culture on the contents of the mind. I believe that this was a profound influence on Freud's thinking.

Freud followed Artemidorus in agreeing with Aristotle that contrary to popular belief, dreams do not come from the gods but from the physiological process. In other words, they come from the body, including the brain, which is, in turn, modified by culture.

Artemidorus used another principle that Freud followed; "Even if a legend is more or less fictitious, our presumption that it is true means that our unconscious mind brings that legend into play whenever it wants to warn us that something analogous to the context of the legend is about happen" (2.66. 1–2).

This influence of the unconscious mind is what all analysts agree on. Brenner (1982) called it the first principle of psychoanalytic thinking. Another principle of Artemidorus is that some dreams simply reflect the dreamer's immediate experiences and/or feelings. Such dreams are the result of what Freud named "day residue."

Another way Freud followed Artemidorus is in setting aside analogy for more specific clues to meaning. Rather than use set symbols, the interpreter uses possible meanings. For Artemidorus these are to be derived from the interpreter's experience. Freud used the patient's experience, rather than the interpreter's, to understand the meaning of a dream element. In Freud's *Interpretation of Dreams,* dreamer and analyst are the same person, so the distinction between the patient's experience and that of the analyst is lost. But in his work with other patients, it is significant. And it has become a standard of analytic practice to inquire about what comes to the patient's mind.

Thonemann (2020) notes that Artemidorus did not follow up his belief that dreams come from the unconscious with an interest in exploring that unconscious. In that way, Freud went beyond his predecessor. Thonemann also points out that while Artemidorus believed that what a dream meant depended on the person who dreamed it. But he looked only at the person insofar as his social status as determined by age, sex, family and occupation. A dream meant one thing if it was dreamed by a slave, something else if it was dreamed by an artisan, and yet something else if it was dreamed by a patrician. Similarly, it had different meanings for a man or woman, and different for a shoemaker than a farmer or a senator. And the age of the dreamer as well as the political conditions at the time affected the meaning of the dream. Was the city at war? Was there a famine? Was the dreamer ambitious, fearful, seeking revenge, looking for love, escaping something or someone? All these status markers, and historical and contextual events, were present and conscious.

But for Freud the dream was determined by personal history. He went beyond Artemidorus in using the analysand's memories of childhood and adolescence as well as current life to understand dreams. Above all, he saw dreams as being driven by unconscious affects, wishes, fears, moral judgements, defenses, and compromises between these.

For both Artemidorus and Freud, word-play, puns, and reversals were part of interpretation. An important technique in interpretation for both Artemidorus and Freud is the use of puns and similar word play. Freud quotes this from Artemidorus.:

"Alexander dreamed he saw a satyr dancing on his shield. Aristander happened to be in the neighborhood of Tyre, in attendance on the king during his Syrian campaign. By dividing the word satyr into óá and rúpaç he encouraged the to press home the siege so that he became master of the city. óá Τύρος = Tyre is thine." (Loc. tk)

Reversals figure in Artemidorus's work as well. Here Freud is in direct agreement with Artemidorus. He refers to Artemidorus way of understanding dreams:

"In interpreting the images seen in dreams, one must sometimes follow them from the beginning to the end, and sometimes from the end to the beginning…" (Loc. 19284). This is in a footnote added in 1914. By using this reference Freud shows that he was still reading and consulting Artemidorus even years after the first publication of his own dream book.

But all interpretations either one makes are interpretations of what is in the mind of the dreamer. For Artemidorus they predict the future; for Freud they express the past.

But for Freud they also affect the future because those affects, wishes, fears, defenses, and moral judgements not only determine dreams, but they also determine thoughts and behavior. Freud asserts that they also determine daydreams and hysterical symptoms:

"Hysterical symptoms are not attached to actual memories, but to phantasies erected on the basis of the basis of memories." (Loc. 22952).

These fantasies are attempts to solve a current problem by reconciling wishes, fears, defenses, and moral judgements. For Freud the mind is working at night just as in the day, but using a different processing system that depends on visual images, puns, condensation, and reversals rather than the verbal logic of daily thought.

For Artemidorus it is important to know that dreams are the product of the dreamer's mind, not communications from the gods (Loc. 4.59.3–4). He proves this by noting that uneducated people do not use literary quotations or allusions in their dreams, but educated people do use such allusions.

But why he be so concerned with this? Predictions in dreams are no less believable if they came from the gods. If he is just claiming to predict the future from dreams he need not make the point that they are creations of the mind of the dreamer. But this is a key point in his thinking. It explains why it is so necessary for the interpreter to know the dreamers' gender, social class, age, profession, and family position.

This way of thinking about dreams becomes key for Freud when he chooses dreams as the surest way into the mind of the dreamer. But he differs from Artemidorus when he thinks about whether dreams are divisible into two categories. Artemidorus separated dreams into those that are instigated by bodily functions and those that were not. He regarded the first category as uninterpretable, while the second had meaning hidden in the symbols in the dream. Freud agreed with him about the second category, but he insisted that all dreams are constructed of wishes and day residues even if they were apparently prompted by physical stimuli like thirst or the need to urinate.

He wrote:

"To put it another way, stimuli arising during sleep are worked-up into a wish fulfillment, the other constituents of which are the familiar psychical day residues" (Loc. 17045).

Artemidorus was interpreting dreams of people who were anxious. Employing a dream interpreter meant the client was worried about the future. The interpreter understood that his forecast would affect the client's state of mind. While Artemidorus records many dreams that predict disasters, he never tells his readers whether he told the client of impending doom. He did not seem interested in averting the disasters that some of his interpretations warned dreamers would happen.

Similarly, Freud interpreted dreams for people who were anxious. His patients came to him worried about their futures. But he read the future from the past in much greater detail than did Artemidorus. Freud's method differs from that of Artemidorus in two ways. First, Freud expected the dreamer to provide associations linking elements of the dream to her conscious thoughts while Artemidorus associated to the elements of the dream himself without asking the dreamer what the elements called up to the dreamer. He went directly from the dream to his view of what it meant. Second, Freud looked to the dream as an outcome of the dreamer's past and clue to current troubles while Artemidorus went straight to the future.

Some classical scholars (Price, S. 2004; Thonemann, P., 2020) believe that Freud's method was more different from Artemidorus than Freud claimed, and that Freud was citing Artemidorus to give his ideas the elevating appearance of classical scholarship. On the contrary, Freud used dreams to uncover hidden wishes. And Artemidorus had shown the way for this. For example, here is Artemidorus on envy, narcissistic over-valuation and fear:

"To dream of enlarging one's estate and possessing a more expansive or even luxurious property, as long as it is more expensive or moderately better than one's existing property, is a good thing. But to dream of riches far beyond any possibility is ominous, and an indication of financial loss. A wealthy man has expenses to meet, and is necessarily exposed to criminal designs and envy—all the rich are plotted against and envied" (Loc. 4–17).

And here he writes of jealousy and aggression:

> "Anything that is always the result of *happenings in real life* must also be the result of happenings in dreams. An example is the painter who dreamt that he had intercourse with his stepmother. After that dream he fell out with his father. That was because any act of adultery results in jealousy and hostility. Accept this principle with all other dreams of well, and you will not go wrong" (Loc. 4–20).

But the most important part of Artemidorus' work is his consideration of sex and gender. For Foucault (tk) the crucial part of Artemidorus's view of sexuality is who penetrates and who is penetrated. According to Thonemann's understanding of Artemidorus: "Sex is 'good' if the relationship penetrator/penetrated corresponds to a relationship of domination/submission outside the bedroom, if not, it is not" (Loc. 1533).

Oral sex is classified as contrary to law which Thonemann interprets as contrary to social custom. Artemidorus's view is that mutual willingness is what makes sex good for both penetrator and penetrated. If is not consensual, it is not good. Sex acts other than penetration by a penis are considered either impossible or uninteresting. And oral sex is not somehow considered penetration, nor is the tongue or the fingers considered capable of penetration. We cannot know whether this view of sex was personal to Artemidorus or was common in his culture, but it seems to have influenced Freud, whose phallocentric views led him to his least realistic theories: his theories about women.

And the subject of sex is where Freud's most important and controversial ideas cluster as well. Dreams for him are, like conflicts, most often about forbidden sexual wishes. In Freud's *The Interpretation of Dreams* he says:

"It is fair to say that there is no group of ideas that is incapable of representing sexual facts and wishes" (Loc. 20228). "Thus, this substance led me to sexuality, the factor to which I attributed the greatest importance in the origin of nervous disorders which it was my aim to cure" (Loc. 14584). He says that dream wishes that are mysterious are so because they are constructed in order to hide these sexual wishes.

How to draw the curtains that conceal these sexual wishes and find what is hidden behind them? Freud gives us a variety of methods. For example, he says:

"A dream caused by stimuli arising the male sex organs may cause the dreamer to find the top part of a clarinet in the street, or the mouthpiece of a tobacco pipe, or, again, a piece of fur. Here the clarinet and the tobacco pipe represent the approximate shape of the male organ, while the fur stands for the pubic hair. In the case of a sexual dream in a woman, the narrow space where the thighs come together may be represented by a narrow courtyard surrounded by houses, while the vagina may be symbolized by a soft, slippery and very narrow footpath leading across the yard along which the dreamer has to pass, in order, perhaps, to take a gentleman a letter" (Loc.14937).

The specificity of these images suggests that they are references to actual dreams the interpreter has been told. This mirrors Artemidorus' emphasis on the experience of the interpreter as the key to symbolism and interpretation. The idea that the male dreams show the male organ, and the female dreams give images of the female organ, is similar to Artemidorus's idea that the sex or status of the dreamer determines the meaning of the symbols in the dream. These principles are to be found in all of the dream interpretations Freud uses in his *Interpretation of Dreams*.

The most important assumption in Freud's *Interpretation of Dreams* is the idea that dreams are products of the mind. He bolsters the credibility of this idea and links it to the notion of dreams as predictors of the future when he says:

"The fact that dreams concern themselves with attempts at solving the problems by which our mental life is faced is no more strange than that our conscious waking life should do so, beyond this, it merely tells us that that activity can also be carried on in the preconscious and this we already knew" (Loc. 23296).

Finding the meaning of a dream is thus dependent on finding the problem the dreamer is attempting to solve: the hidden problem.

In his *Interpretation of Dreams* Freud devotes a whole chap-ter to symbols in dreams. He cites Artemidorus Book 11,

Chapter 10: "Thus for instance, a bedchamber stands for a wife, if such there be in the house." (Loc. 19992). He uses this as evidence for the rooms in a house symbolizing women. In this, Artemidorus and Freud both use symbols as common references but limit their use by choosing the context in which they occur. Furthermore, Freud uses the experience of psychoanalysts of using dream symbols in interpretations. This is a direct mirroring of Artemidorus is key to understanding dreams. Both Artemidorus and Freud constantly caution readers to rely on experience derived from interpreting dreams to understand the dream at hand.

He relates dream symbols to an ancient belief. He says:

"For with the help of a knowledge of dream symbolism, it is possible to understand the meaning of separate elements of the content of a dream or separate pieces of a dream, or in some cases, even whole dreams, without having to ask the dreamer for his associations. Here we are approaching the popular ideal of translating dreams and on the other hand are returning to the technique of interpretation used by the ancients, to whom dream interpretation was identical with interpretation by means of symbols." (Loc. 26735).

From Artemidorus Freud could infer that interest in dreams was universal, concur that dreams come from the mind, and infer that there was meaning hidden in the symbolic mechanisms of dream construction that could lead an interpreter of dreams to find the hidden meaning. He cites Artemidorus's method of interpreting the dream by examining each image in it separately, rather than trying to understand it as a whole. In addition, the interpreter could know that the meaning was expressed by the mind of the dreamer so the more one knew about the dreamer's life, experiences, hopes, fears, and moral standards, the better one could interpret dreams. And, on the other hand, the more one understood a dream, the better one could understand the mind of the dreamer. All of this led Freud to give dreams the extraordinary place he gave them in the technique of psychoanalysis.

Although he used this method for interpreting dreams, Freud chose to use the same method to understand jokes, psychoses, and neurotic symptoms. He says: "Ideas in dreams and in psychoses have in common the characteristic of being *fulfillments of wishes*. My own researches have taught me that in this fact lies the key to psychological theory of both dreams and psychoses" (Loc. 14050).

A crucial part of the interpretation, both for Artemidorus and Freud, is the separation between manifest and latent content of a dream. Thus, for Freud, a dream of seeing her younger nephew dead as his elder brother turns out to mean that the dreamer wants to see the young man who came to mourn the older brother again. It is not a dream of malice towards the younger nephew.

In the end Freud apologists for not giving more attention to manifestly sexual dreams:

> "Moreover, the moral judgement by which the Translator of *The Oneirocritica* of Artemidorus of Daldis allowed himself to be led into withholding the chapter on sexual dreams from the knowledge of his readers strikes me as laughable. What governed my decision was simply my seeing that an explanation of sexual dreams would involve me deeply in the still unsolved problems of perversion and bisexuality; and I accordingly reserved this material for another occasion" (Loc. 25377).

Here we get a glimpse of the extent to which Freud valued Artemidorus's discussion of sexual dreams and wishes and yet lived in a social setting in which such things were not to be investigated or discussed even by scholars. Freud never actually made good on his promise to discuss dreams involving perverse or bisexual wishes. We can only speculate that using sexual dreams of his own would be too revealing or embarrassing in that social climate. Artemidorus was not using his own dreams, or, at least, not stating that any of the dreams he wrote about were his own. And he lived in a time and place where sexuality was not so severely repressed. He frankly discussed dreams of sexual positions, adultery, same sex sexual partners, incest, and sex with animals.

Freud's apology suggests that he regarded such dreams as worthy of attention, but not at that moment. Since he begins this footnote by condemning the Translator for eliminating the chapter on dreams with manifest sexual content, he seems to be defending himself from his own accusation of himself for writing like the Translator rather than like Artemidorus. And it is possible that he did not believe he could get any farther than Artemidorus in understanding that those dreams were manifestly sexual, but based on a wish for power.

Yet Freud does describe dreams as concealing sexual wishes so that even if sex is not evident in the manifest dream, it is the latent dream wish. And he considers the study of dreams to be central to his entire psychoanalytic project. He says:

> "Thus, I would look for the theoretical value of the study of dreams in the contributions it makes to psychological knowledge and in the preliminary light it throws on the problems of the psychoneuroses. Who can guess the importance of the results which might be obtained from a thorough understanding of the structure and functions of the mental apparatus since even the present stage of our knowledge allows us to exert a therapeutic influence on the curable forms of psychoneurosis?" (Loc. 25636).

Conclusions

The things Freud found in Artemidorus work meshed nicely with the method of using associations that he had used with neurotic patients in order to understand their symptoms. Did he get them initially from Artemidorus? I cannot say. I do not know when he first read his work. What is clear is that he agreed with much of it. I think modern psychoanalysts think of associations not as a linear series, but as part of a complex webbing the brain, closer to the spiderweb than to the line from which she suspends that web. The first association that comes to mind may or may not be the key to the meaning of the scene in the dream, much less the key to the whole dream. So that while Freud's idea of interpreting the dream was to find the wish that fueled the dream, modern psychoanalysts also understand dreams as communications to the person to whom they are told, or consolidations of daily experience, or using current experience to modify understandings derived from infantile experience, we also understand the dream as a multidetermined, and multifunctional activity of the mind driven by emotion.

As a practicing analyst, I do know that I think of the person's past as prelude to the present and the present as prelude to the future. I do not go in for backward fortune telling. I aim to influence the person's future satisfaction with life by helping them to understand and therefore modify those behaviors that bring them grief. As Freud saw it then, and as I see it now, past pushes feelings and thought, feelings and thought push fantasy, dreams, and daydreams. Fantasy shapes future behavior because fantasy is the wish embodied in a story and that story can become reality. Once we know our wishes, we can work on making them come true.

References

Artemidorus. (2020) *Oneirocritica: The Interpretation of Dreams.* Tr. M. Hammond. Oxford: Oxford Univ. Press. Kindle Books.

Brenner, C. (1982). *The Mind in Conflict.* New York: International Universities Press.

Freud, S. (1905) The Interpretation of Dreams. In: *Complete Works.* Kindle Books.

Price, S. (2004) The Future of Dreams: From Freud to Artemidorus, In*: Studies in Ancient Greek and Roman Society.* ed. R. Osborne, p. 226–259.

Thonemann, M. (2020) *An Ancient Dream Manual.* Oxford: Oxford Univ. Press. Kindle Books.

Yu, H. (2001). *China in Ten WORDS.* New York: Pantheon. Kindle Books.

Dreams in Clinical Works

Edward Nersessian

In lecture XXIX of "The New Introductory Lectures" Freud lamented the disappearance from the *International Journal of Psychoanalysis* of the section entitled "On Dream Interpretation," and the fact that "analysts behaved as though there was nothing more to say about dreams, as though there was no more to be added to the theory of dreams." Now one hundred years since *The Interpretation of Dreams* it may be useful to consider the fate of the study of dreams in psychoanalysis. I will speak here only as a so-called classical analyst, which in this country means those who continue to adhere to Freud's theories and their subsequent development through the works of Hartmann, Kris, Lowenstein, Arlow, and Brenner. My education has been in what is commonly labeled the American Ego Psychology School and its modification by Brenner leading to Modern Conflict Theory.

Prior to embarking on describing a personal view of the fate of dreams, I would like to say a word about another interest of mine, which is the newly emergent dialogue between psychoanalysts and neuroscientists. I hope that over time new insights will ensue from this important exchange, leading to a better understanding of the three aspects of dream theory elaborated in *The Interpretation of Dreams,* which is to say, the function of dreams, the meaning of dreams, and the dream as an entry point for research on the workings of the mind-brain. As you know, many theories abound as to the function of dreams. Yet we do not possess a fuller understanding beyond that which Freud said, namely. that the dream serves to protect sleep or to be more precise to protect the "wish" to.

While most dream researchers (including the psychoanalyst Chuck Fisher) dispute this role for dreams, to my knowledge nothing conclusive has been determined about why we dream, though it is quite likely that dreaming has a larger role in mental functioning than was anticipated by Freud. For example, research on affects and memory may, in the not-too-distant future reveal the role dreaming plays in various aspects of these properties of the mind. Naturally, the function of sleep itself needs to be fully elaborated and understanding sleep may contribute to the understanding of dreaming.

As to the meaning of dreams, our psychoanalytic view has come under serious attack over the past three decades, mostly from work done on REM sleep by the Harvard researcher Hobson and others. It is encouraging that Hobson no longer considers dreams as meaningless, but instead thinks that salient memories and emotions serve as the primary shaper of dream plots. Disagreement remains, however, about the psychoanalytic idea that in a dream a wish is represented as fulfilled. My own training as a psychoanalyst combined with my readings in the neurosciences have me to think that dreams probably play a role in managing affects. especially the so-called negative affects.

Whatever the eventual resolution as the function and meaning of dreams, I firmly believe that we will all benefit from a sustained dialogue between psychoanalysts and neuroscientists, particularly in terms of elucidating the workings of the brain-mind. Recent brain imaging studies are showing great promise in this area, by demonstrating, for example, the areas of the brain that show more activity during dreaming (see Braun).

This summarizes some currents in the developing understanding of dreams taking place outside of psychoanalysis, within psychoanalysis, and particularly within my own school, I could schematically describe two trends. First, up until the late 50s, there was a move towards supplementing Freud's ideas, spear-headed by Otto Isakower and Bertram Lewin. In the years that followed, a second trend emerged, diminishing the emergence of dreams both in clinical work and in psychoanalytic theory. Arlow and Brenner initially advanced this which was later enlarged upon by Brenner. All four of these clinician theorists have been important teachers at my institution, the New York Psychoanalytic Institute, and their writings form the backdrop from which my views on dreams in clinical practice have emerged,

Let me say right away that for my part, I continue to find dream analysis extremely useful. I am gratified with the help they sometimes provide and hope with the three brief examples that follow to demonstrate their usefulness. Naturally, not all dreams lend themselves to analysis and not all patients work with dreams in the same way. Additionally, what constitutes a useful analysis of a dream also varies greatly. In my experience, dreams that lend themselves to the kind of analysis Freud demonstrated with his botanical monograph dream are rare but do occur with some patients who seem particularly curious about their dreams. Lest anyone suspect these particular patients are students in psychoanalysis, let me dispel that notion. In my experience, people who are very knowledgeable about psychoanalysis report dreams regularly but rarely actually want to analyze them. Parenthetically, I would add that my own ability to contribute to a dream analysis also varies and seems to be not only a function of what I know about the patient, the context, the day residue, but also the particular state of mind I am in, and the affective curiosity aroused in me by the dream. I do not know whether others share this feeling, but from experience I can see myself more or less interested in a dream, while remaining curious about the rest of the material. At times, such countertransference reactions can be profitably analyzed, but at other times they remain limited to one particular dream and are left unattended. It is also to say that one does not wish to analyze all dreams thoroughly and especially in the early phases of an analysis, it is sometimes prudent not to bring out all the latent themes that can be detected, in order not to arouse too much anxiety or excessive defensive intellectualization. Furthermore, it is important not to come across as wizard of dream analysis early in a treatment, this can have problematic consequences.

With these introductory comments, I will now present three vignettes. None of these examples demonstrate an exhaustive analysis of dreams, which as I have already indicated seldom happens, nor are particularly unusual; instead, I hope they show the usefulness of dreams in the every day work of analysis.

Prior to reporting the first example I would like to say a word about transference, which is often the focus in most dream reports in seminars and published papers. There is little or no doubt that in ongoing analysis the transference will inevitably appear in the dream that the person of the analyst, a transference figure, distorted in the customary ways, will frequently be present. Since the analysis and analyst are often in the day residue. this is not surprising. I think, however, that we fail to take sufficient advantage of what dreams can offer if we do not attempt to go beyond and even beside the obvious manifestations of the transference. Too often, as soon as the evidence for the transference is detected in a given dream, it is interpreted. and all other potentially rich material is ignored.

I hope the example that follows illustrates this point. I should warn the audience by saying that the elements of an erotic transference are so clear, that whoever has heard this dream has focused almost exclusively on it, but I would like to suggest that, though present, other affects were stronger.

Example 1: The patient was a young married woman, with one young son, who had been in analysis for three years at the time of this dream. She had a great need to be in control and put up a cheerful, intellectual, and friendly attitude to defend against intense inner emotions. One of her complaints was that since the birth of her son she did not enjoy sex with her husband very much, but on the day before the dream, she so enjoyed sex with him that they had intercourse twice. That night she dreamt that she was climbing up a cold white marble statue of a young male, and when she began sucking on the white and very smooth testicles of the statue, it slowly carne to life.

The patient was then somewhat cheerful in the session and talked in the same upbeat way about her ongoing anger and jealousy of her husband who had surpassed her in professional success in the same field as they both practiced. From there, her thoughts went to my upcoming week-long vacation, and since it was during spring break for the New York City schools, she assumed I was going away with my family and children. She especially focused on a daughter she imagined I have and towards whom she believed I was very loving and affectionate. Not at all like the distant and cold professional I was towards her. She also reported talking to her mother the day of the dream. The mother, who had breast cancer, had complained about some aches and pains which had worried the patient in a passing way as to their possibly metastatic origin. but which she had later dismissed as just being the usual pains of old age or possibly a flu.

Naturally, I thought that perhaps the dream was expressing her feelings about my lack of affectionate availability to her, with the desire to transform me from a cold psychoanalyst to a warm, aroused, lively lover. I was struck, however, by her description of the texture and color of the testicles. Knowing her intense fear of the loss of her only surviving, highly ambivalently loved parent and her inability to deal with the inevitability of this loss except through mild hypomanic defenses and an intense need to control all emotions, I chose not to interpret what seemed to me as the more obvious transference meaning of the dream. Instead, I asked her if she was very worried about her mother, whom she knew had metastatic cancer in the bone and whom she wished she could keep alive. Somewhat to my surprise and for only the second or third time in the analysis, the patient began sobbing intensely and talked about the unfairness of it all. She revealed, while sadly crying, a series of fantasies about her mother's death, the funeral arrangements, whether her mother would be alive the next New Year and so on. Prior to this point, none of these fantasies had been available to the analysis and concerns about the mother's health had either been minimized or dealt with in a very matter of fact manner.

I will interrupt this report here and once again stress that an excessive focus on the transference may obscure other useful avenues of exploration in the dream. I am not trying to oversimplify and to ignore how various issues are related, but instead to highlight the need to be parsimonious in interpreting a dream, and in doing so, hopefully to touch on what is affectively most charged at the moment.

My next vignette has to do with the observation that there are times when a dream helps bring to light a childhood memory which has remained out of the patient's awareness up to that point.

Example 2: A man in his early thirties who had been in treatment for less than a year at the time the following dream was reported initially presented with a depressed mood accompanied by obsessive fears about the well being of his loved ones, Extremely intelligent and a good observer of the world around him , he had rather severe inhibition about observing the world within; in other words. he had more voyeurism than curiosity and communicated with people with difficulty, He also had sex on his mind all the time.

"I am in this house, upstairs, and the room I am in is green. I am with a woman. and then there seems to be a danger, like the color green becomes dangerous, and we have to escape, and I wake up."

Associations: I visited my parents over the weekend with my wife and went upstairs to the apartment my aunt and her husband used to rent in our house when I was a kid. I was trying to see if it was as I remembered it or not. We were there for Mothers' Day, and my mom was happy that we went. That afternoon, I started thinking of J. and wondering if I should call her and wish her a happy Mother's Day. (J. is a woman he is very attracted to and has been very flirtatious with.) I decided not to because if my wife ever found out, she would kill me.

Analyst: In your dream you were with a woman, and there was danger.

Patient: I didn't think about it that way. It was the green color that was dangerous, and I can't imagine why I would be afraid of a color.

Analyst: Does the color bring anything to mind?

Patient: It is my mother's favorite color. In our house when I was growing up, everything was green … walls, curtains, bedspreads. Not upstairs though, only in our part of the house. My mother also loves plants, so we had plants everywhere. but my aunt didn't have any because they only lived upstairs a few months a year. I remember when they were away, I would go up there and play. In high school, I would go there with girls and fool around, but my mother never caught us. When I was much younger, 8–9 years old, I would play doctor with our next door neighbor's daughter who was my age, but I don't remember doing that upstairs. They had a big back yard, and we would go there and take our clothes off.

Following session:

Patient: had another dream. I was in my country house. There was a station wagon. I was in the station wagon and there was someone else in it.

Associations: My car is not a station wagon, but my parents used to have one when I was a kid. I remember when I was 8 or 9 years old we took a long cross country trip in that car. I loved that trip, it's funny, but what comes to mind is that one time my mother was very angry at me during the trip. My sister (two years younger) and I were in the back of the station wagon, and I think we had taken our clothes off under a blanket. and I asked her to touch my penis, and my mother heard it and was furious. Maybe the dangerous green is my mother. (Laughs)

Analyst: So, did you also play doctor with your sister?

Patient: Oh, a lot. We were very sexual together when we were young, but I don't remember where we did that. I clearly remember the backyard with the neighbor, but with my sister I don't seem to picture a place except that time in the car. But I just know we fooled around a lot.

Analyst: Could it have been upstairs?

Patient: Could have been. I don't remember being upstairs with my sister.

In the next and last vignette, I think we see the interrelationship between transference, memory, and dreams. Here. what was difficult for the patient to become aware of in the here and now brought into consciousness a memory about a repetitive occurrence in childhood which then facilitated getting in touch with his transference feelings.

Example 3: The session was after the weekend, and Ms., C. began reporting on a fight she had with a good male friend, G. A woman, L, who was a mutual friend was staying with her and C. had arranged to meet L. on Saturday evening. My patient, upon hearing this, decided to accompany L. to the meeting, and G. was very upset. He felt that he was friendly with L. independent of C. and should be able to spend an evening with her alone. This story occupied a good part of the hour, but then the patient stopped, and after a brief silence said: I had a dream last night, "You will think it significant. It is the kind of dream shrinks think is important."

After a few more similar qualifying comments, she reported the following dream: She was in a bathroom. It was very large and steamed up. I was there, and I told her to get undressed, that I wanted her naked. I was naked, but she did not really look, the way she always avoids looking at naked people. The situation was sexually very arousing. In real lite, she would find such a situation—a man ordering her to take her clothes off—very exciting. She then went back to discussing the weekend events further, and then, changing the subject, she said.

"I have been thinking about what you said in the last session. I agree that I want to be special here and feel my relationship with you is different than with your other patients. I realized that when I had complained to you about my breasts and that they are deformed and too small and not firm, I was excited by it. I felt as if I were showing myself to you naked. I was craving your attention to my body."

In order to clarify the context of this material and the dream, it should he added that some two weeks earlier she had reported from the time that when she was between the ages of 7–8 to 11–12 on a number of occasions she would be taking bath in her parents' bathroom (the only bathroom in the house with a tub), and her father would walk in naked to take a shower in the shower room, which was behind the head of the tub. At the time she had reported this, she had not recalled any other feeling except that "well that is how it was in our house" and a certain mild annoyance. Yet in the transference with me whenever sexual matters carne up, she would feel disgusted towards me and think me as a disgusting, dirty old man. The dream not only helped bring together many of the issues we have been struggling with, but most importantly it brought forth an awareness of her own wishes and desires and made possible for her to recognize the ongoing influence of her childhood experience in her current fantasies both within the analysis but also in the outside world.

Last year we celebrated the hundredth-year anniversary of the publication of *The Interpretation of Dreams*. I hope it is clear from the above that now, a century later, I continue to benefit in my work from the help offered to me by dreams. And I predict that dreams have many more insights left to offer to psychoanalysts and to all interested in the study of mind-brain

---

.

Are Dreams "The Royal Road to the Unconscious"?

Charles P. Fisher

August 13, 2021

Freud famously wrote that *"The interpretation of dreams is the royal road to a knowledge of the unconscious activities of the mind* (Freud, 1900, p. 608), What is less well known is that he immediately added in a footnote:

> Dreams are not the only phenomena which allow us to find a basis for psychopathology in psychology. In a short series of papers (1898b and 1899a) which is not yet completed, I have attempted to interpret a number of phenomena of daily life as evidence in favor of the same conclusions [*Added* 1909]. These, together with some further papers on forgetting, slips of the tongue, bungled actions, etc., have since been collected under the title of *The Psychopathology of Everyday Life* (Freud, 1901b).

Eugene Mahon's essay "Dreams Within Dreams" (Mahon 2004) moves me to add that another "royal road to the unconscious" is the psychoanalytic interaction between a brilliant and talented analysand and a brilliant and talented psycho-analyst in the termination phase of a successful analysis. Mr. P's dream is not only a source of knowledge about his unconscious mental life (and about dreams within dreams). It is also a product of collaboration between patient and analyst over a period of years, and especially within the process of termination of the analysis. In Eugene Mahon's pellucid article, we have his written account of the dream as narrated by Mr. P, along with associations offered by Mr. P in the analytic hour and by Dr. Mahon in the course of preparing his article.

Mahon writes:

> I am suggesting that once there has been a feeling of the uncanny in waking life, what's to stop dream life from recycling it unconsciously and reprising it in dream life as a dream within a dream? Surely it is this kind of uncanny recycling that the poet tries to capture when he says, "*La vida es sueño.,*" (Calderón de la Barca 1636) or "our little life is rounded with a sleep" (Shakespeare 1564–1616). If this implies an even greater continuity between dream life and waking life than is usually thought of, a reciprocal cross-fertilization of one by the other, it may also highlight a cultural mistrust of the oneiric in Occidental circles, Oriental culture being far less discriminating when it comes to distinguishing dream life from waking life, as the title of Wendy Doniger O'Flaherty's (1984), astute study, "Dreams, Illusion, and Other Realities," suggests, (Mahon 2024, p. 11).

I will pick up on the relationship between dreaming and reality shortly. At this juncture, my point is that the analyst's observations while writing about the patient's dream *also* count as associations to the dream. In saying this, I am seeing the dream report itself as a shared creative product arising from the dyad's work of eight years' duration. Mr. P had a dream during the night, recalled an unconsciously edited version of it in an analytic session, and reported that version within the context of an intense transference relationship which had considerable history to it. That history, within Mr. P's conscious, preconscious, and unconscious memory, provided materials used in the dream. In Eugene Mahon's article, we receive an account of how the analyst heard the dream and presented it to readers. As Thomas Ogden wrote, "The dream dreamt in the course of an analysis is in a sense the dream of the analytic third," (Ogden, 1996, p. 884), in other words a co-construction. And the analyst's writing is in itself part of a dynamic process. As Robert Michels wrote in "The Case History," (Michels, 2000, p. 371) "Every analyst presenting a case is like the candidate with a first case, and every case presentation, like analysis itself, is theater as well as report, with the analyst-presenter an actor as well as author, whose performance as presenter provides an important insight into his or her performance as analyst." Taking my point one step further, writing about a case becomes part of the analyst's personal work, parallel to a patient's personal consolidation of analytic work after termination. I am extending Michels' point a bit to suggest that Eugene Mahon's textual associations while writing about Mr. P's dream also count as associations to the co-constructed dream which occurred in Mr. P's analysis. Hence, when Mahon mentions "*La vida es sueño*" and "Dreams, Illusion, and Other Realities," these references count as associations to Mr. P's analytic dream. "Reality," illusion, and the dream-within-a-dream are on a par with one another in the world of the psychoanalytic dream. I will add that "Reality," as it appears within the context of psychoanalysis is also a "royal road to the unconscious."

But first, I would like to comment on a central thesis in Mahon's article, and about his clinical case formulation. Mahon places emphasis "on *both* portions" of the dream-within-a-dream process "and the dynamic links between them," (p. 13, this volume). I strongly agree with him when he states that, "By drawing attention to 'the dynamic linkage between the two portions of the dream sequence I believe that the multiple determinants of both are enriched and high-lighted" (p. 13, this volume). His case illustration provides convincing and elegant evidence of this point. This evidence sounds like science, rather than dogma (to invert Mahon's comment about Freud's lack of clinical evidence on the issue of the dream-within-a-dream).

I believe that Mahon's summary of Mr. P's dream thoughts (p. 7, this volume) is convincing, but under-emphasizes two points. The first is a specifically homo-erotic aspect to the dream and the transference. While Mahon does write about Mr. P's wish to have a baby with him, he omits the notion of a specifically sexual fantasy about their relationship. This theme is reflected in the historical piece about the patient's memory of being punished for urinating while in bed with his father. The theme of the bearded man in the dream is accompanied by Mahon's emphasis that neither the father nor the analyst had a beard. It does not seem like a stretch to point out that the New Oxford Dictionary of English contains the alternative definition of a "beard" as "a woman who dates, or marries, a gay man to provide cover for the man's homosexuality," (downloaded 8/13/2021).

The second point which I see as undermphasized is the trauma of telling. Mahon writes, "By putting trauma in one dream and "telling" in a dream within it, the analysand was declaring that 'telling' was as great a trauma as trauma itself, and that the two should not be confused" (p. 8, this volume). This way of putting it simultaneously states that "telling" was a trauma and diminishes it by comparison with the "trauma itself." But within the transference relationship, it was the opportunity for "telling" that was about to be painfully lost with termination. The urination, within the patient's memory, can stand for the more immediate reality of a stream of associations. Telling is not just telling, but an expression of love, including erotic love, in the face of inevitable loss. Hence, in the analytic moment described here, telling may have been the more painful trauma.

I'd like to turn now to the topic of reality. I've mentioned earlier that there are many royal roads to the unconscious, including dreams and the process of psychoanalysis itself. Freud notably added symptoms and transference, as well as "forgetting, slips of the tongue, bungled actions, etc. ..." Today, we might add countertransference. And now, I would like to add "reality" itself, as it is presented within psycho-analysis. Loewald wrote, "Ego, id and external reality become distinguishable in their most primitive, germinal stages. This state of affairs can be expressed either by saying that 'the ego detaches itself from the external world', or, more correctly: the ego detaches from itself an outer world. Originally the ego contains everything" (Loewald, 1951, p. 11). This is not simply a philosophical point. The construction of perceptual "reality" within the mind is well supported by the evidence underlying Mark Solms' recent comment about the apparent stability of visual perception: "The stabilized scene also hints at the fact that what we perceive is just that—a *scene*—a con-structed perspective upon reality, not reality itself" (Solms, 2021, p. 140). In Solms' recent book, *The Hidden Spring*, this comment is extended to describe all of reality as a constructed perspective. In psychoanalysis, "Reality," as a construct, is an emotional truth, as well as a literal one. Eugene Mahon al-ludes to this concept in his authorial associations to Mr. P's dream—or I should say the dream as jointly constructed by patient and analyst near the end of an eight-year analysis.

My professional experience includes what Mahon refers to as "an even greater continuity between dream life and wak-ing life than is usually thought of a reciprocal cross-fertiliza-tion of one by the other... ." (p. 11, this volume). With my colleague, Beth Kalish, I have studied the dream-interpreting practices of the Achuar people, an indigenous group in the Amazon rainforest. The Achuar practice is to arise daily be-fore dawn every day to share dreams with one another, to interpret their dreams, and to use their dream interpreta-tions to make plans for the day's activities. On many visits to the rainforest, Beth and I have joined small and large groups of Achuar dream interpreters to learn how their practices resemble and differ from the ways that North American psychoanalysts use dreams (Fisher and Kalish, 2011; Kalish and Fisher, 2021; Fisher and Kalish, in preparation; Goldsmith, Fisher, and Kalish, 2020.).

Here is an overview of our conclusions to date, as they have affected us as analysts:

* For the Achuar, dreams are more real than waking reality. When interpreted, they are a more reliable guide to action than waking thoughts. While this conclusion is easy to state, it is quite difficult for a person raised in North American culture to comprehend this worldview on a practical level. However, this perspective provides a useful orientation to psychic reality. Beth and I are now more likely to look at "reality," as presented in analysis, as being in itself a product constructed like a dream.

* Dreams are thought to predict the future. This concept, dismissed by Freud as primitive folklore, has meaning to Beth and me in relation to our own practices of psychoanalysis. We see our patients' dreams, and our own, as reflecting wishes and predictions involving the dreamer's unconscious intentions, expected consequences of action upon those intentions, and unformulated perceptions about the world—the "unthought known." We are more likely to see dreams as predictive of emotion and action.

* Dreams are interpreted in a social context, which consists of both the immediate dream-sharing group and the larger social reality of the community in which the dream-sharing takes place. The social context in which the dream will be reported enters into the dream itself. This occurs because the dreamer already has the anticipated audience in mind (as preconscious day residues) forming background material for the dream. Beth and I have come to see that analysts practicing psychoanaly-

sis (as well as our patients) are participants in thought collectives that actively guide our clinical work. We have in mind psychoanalytic study groups, training programs, consultants, societies, schools of thought, conferences, and the like for analysts, and numerous cultural groups for patients. Like the Achuar, our interpretations are also group interpretations—dreamer and interpreter are engaged in the shared meanings of a small group (of two), within the shared meanings of larger psychoanalytic and cultural groups. As a result of our experiences with the Achuar, Beth and I are more likely to reflect upon these shared meanings as constitutive of patients' dreams and our own responses to them.

For me, these conclusions, based on our observations about Achuar dream interpretation, apply to Eugene Mahon's clinical report in certain ways:

* They support Mahon's thesis that both parts of Mr. P's dream are important and that they mutually illuminate each other. Both parts refer to "reality" as a special kind of dream, as well as referring to each other.

* They support the conclusion that the near-future termination of the analysis, as well as the remote-past of the father's anger about the patient's urination, are part of the psychically immediate present, which is forcefully represented in the dream.

* They support the conclusion that Mr. P's dream is a shared creative product of the analytic dyad, summarizing years of work.

* They support the conclusion that Mahon's article can be viewed, in part, as a continuing associative process on the part of the analyst, illuminating the shared meaning of the dream, and constituting a part of the analyst's work, to deal with the loss of the patient and the analysis, and to integrate what the analyst himself has gained from the experience.

Conclusion

Eugene Mahon's beautiful article illustrates the fact that dreams are *a* royal road to the unconscious, but not *the* royal road to the unconscious.

References

Calderón de la Barca, P. (1636). *La vida es sueño*. Denver: University Press of Colorado. 2004.

Doniger O'Flaherty, W. (1984). *Dreams, Illusion, and Other Realities*. Chicago: University of Chicago Press.

Fisher, C.P. & Kalish, B. (2011). Dreaming and Reality: A Comparison of Interpretive Work in Two Cultures: North American Psychoanalysis and an Indigenous Culture in the Amazon Rainforest. Presented at the January 2011 meeting of the American Psychoanalytic Association.

———— & ———— (In preparation). *Amazon Dreaming: A Psychoanalytic Exploration of Dream Interpretation Practices in the Ecuadorian Rainforest*. Routledge/Karnac.

Freud, S. (1900). The Interpretation of Dreams. *Standard Edition* 4:ix–627.

———— (1901). The Psychopathology of Everyday Life. *The Standard Edition* 6:vii–296.

Goldsmith, P., Fisher, C.P., & Kalish, B. (2020). The Achuar in the Amazon. A film, available for viewing upon request to Fisher and Kalish.

Kalish, B. & Fisher, C.P. (2021). The Infantile and the Creative in Dreams and Culture. Presented at the 2021 Congress of the International Psychoanalytical Association.

Loewald, H.W. (1951). Ego and Reality. *Int. J. Psycho-Anal.*, 32:10–18.

Mahon, E.J. (2002). Dreams Within Dreams. *Psychoanal. St. Child*, 57:118–130.

Michels, R. (2000). The Case History. *J. Amer. Psychoanal. Assn.*, 48(2):355–375.

Ogden, T.H. (1996). Reconsidering Three Aspects of Psychoanalytic Technique. *Int. J. Psycho-Anal.*, 77:883–899.

Shakespeare, W. (1564–1616). *The Tempest.* Cambridge: Harvard Univ. Press, 1958.

Solms, M. (2021). *The Hidden Spring: A Journey to the Source of Consciousness.* New York: W. W. Norton & Co.

Dreams within Dreams or Ambiguous, Partial Awakenings?

Brent Willock

Abstract

This article complements and challenges current comprehension of dreams within dreams. It identifies a need to be more rigorous regarding the essential elements and boundaries defining this concept and to provide greater contextual detail in presenting such phenomena and our work with them. Sometimes what is reported as a dream nested in a dream may be better understood as a partial or actual awakening. Dreams of all sorts provide an analytically valuable "third" that analysts and patients can contemplate, associate to, and strive to figure out collaboratively. The author concurs with those who, like Freud, continue to find these nocturnal hallucinations to be a royal road to understanding unconscious processes.

I, Zhuang Zhou, dreamt I was a butterfly, fluttering hither and thither, to all intents and purposes a butterfly. I was conscious only of my happiness as a butterfly, unaware that I was Zhou. Soon I awaked, and there I was, veritably myself again. Now I do not know whether I was then a man dreaming I was a butterfly, or whether I am now a butterfly, dreaming I am a man.

–Zhuang Zhou (c. 369 BC–286 BC)

In his intriguing paper, "Dreams Within Dreams," Eugene Mahon (2002) has contributed, with considerable literary style, to the growing literature on this fascinating topic. During the termination phase of his 8-year analysis with Mr. Perdu, a 56-year-old philosophy professor, formerly a priest, who grew up in South Africa, the following dream emerged:

> I awake at the sound of a car pulling into the driveway of our Connecticut house. It is pitch dark, but a child is being dropped off as if our home were a nursery school. All this seemed natural in dream experience even though the time, the darkness, would have been highly unusual for such a drop-off in real time. The scene shifts. I am now outside my house but lost, trying to find my bearings. A child on a bicycle guides me home. Then I walk from my house in Connecticut to Greenwich Village, which in dream geography seems no more than a hundred yards. I am so surprised by the spatial novelty of Connecticut's [being] a stone's throw from Greenwich Village that I wake up, an illusion, as I will discover on actual awakening. In Greenwich Village I walk into a wood-lined office in a townhouse. A bearded man, not unlike the young Freud in the Freud-Fliess era, greets me. I start to tell him the unusual dream I've just had about being lost and how it was a child who guided me home.

Mahon believed that a crucial latent dream thought that entered this dream concerned a trauma in Perdu's childhood that he had recounted early in his analysis. As a child of 5 or 6 years, Perdu had been playing with older boys who suddenly went about their own business, forgetting the younger one who had been entrusted to their care. A kind gentleman on a bicycle rode Perdu home. In later years, whenever this incident was recalled, his mother railed against the boy to whom she had entrusted her son, taking little responsibility for her own negligence. Perdu was aware that in the dream, the bike-riding child who guided him home reversed the roles of child and adult 50 years earlier. Through intensive work with this memory over the years, they had come to understand it as a screen memory that contained and hid the greater reality of maternal and paternal neglect.

In accord with Freud's idea about dreams within dreams, Mahon reasoned that the memory of a painful piece of reality (that childhood trauma) began to surface during the dream. It had to be disavowed and located in a new setting (a dream-within-a-dream) given that the original dream setting was endangered by this emerging presence. Using the cinematographic image of "reel switching," Mahon suggests by changing reels at that moment and seeming to begin a new dream, the content of the first reel was being designated as a dream-within-a-dream in order to disavow the reality that had appeared too undisguisedly in the dream. A piece of historic truth threatened the soothing, sleep-enhancing narrative truth of the dream and needed to be relegated to the status of "not real" by the dream-within-dream strategy, as if to insist that "it's only a dream" needed the added reinforcement of "it's only a dream-within-a-dream. How could I ever have mistaken it for reality?"

Analyst and analysand engaged in complex discussions about which dream was internal to which. Paraphrasing Freud, Perdu commented: "One hides in a dream-within-a-dream an actual event. In that case, depending on which of the dreams is within the other, being lost could be the disavowed actuality, or is it 'telling' about it that is the significant reality that is being relegated to dream life, doubly displaced and captioned as non-real in its dream-within-dream status?" Contemplating his analysand's cogitations, Mahon remarked that the illusion of waking up and telling the dream to a bearded man in Greenwich Village would seem to be the part of the dream that is within the other, larger, earlier part. However, he continued, one could argue that the first part is being told again in the later dream and is therefore "within" it, making the analysand's question not as "intellectual" as it seemed at first blush.

The dream-within-a-dream concept can sometimes be confusing, as the previous paragraph suggests. For a different, complementary, simpler perspective, one might approach this material from the viewpoint of partial *awakenings*, rather than focusing on dreams within dreams. Accenting this possibility is the main *raison d'être* of this article.

Mahon attends to the striking moment when Perdu thought he woke up, startled about Connecticut being unexpectedly close to Greenwich Village, only to discover later, when he actually awoke, that it all that had been a dream. Beyond that dramatic instance of illusory awakening on the road to Greenwich, consider this patient's opening, tone-setting sentence: "I awake at the sound of a car pulling into the driveway." It was not just in the middle of the dream or at its second phase, but from the get-go, that this dream hints that it is about "waking." In both instances, these supposed awakenings turn out to be "waking" into further dreaming. Such material challenges us, providing opportunities to explore the way states of consciousness emerge and merge.

Mahon stated that by putting trauma in one dream and "telling" someone about the trauma in a dream within it, the analysand was declaring that "telling" was as great a trauma as the trauma itself, and that the two should not be confused. Given that both those events were framed within different sorts of alleged dream *awakenings*, one might see these traumas as being held in states of partial, illusory, or faint awakening rather that doubly buried by dreaming within dreaming.

Freud offered that his discipline's core concerns transference and resistance. To the (considerable) extent that his definition of his treatment method is insightful and useful, it underscores the importance of coming to comprehend our transferences so that we can perceive reality closer to what it is, as opposed to what we impose upon it in terms of our organizing principles, defenses, etc. In successful analyses, we emerge from somewhat dreamlike states into something closer to actuality. This can be seen as awakening, or even rebirth (Willock, 2017). For Chinese Taoist philosopher Zhuang Zhou (cited in the epigraph above), the supreme goal in life is to experience the Great Awakening after which one is aware that all that preceded had been, in a sense, a dream.

Perdu's dream arose during analytic termination—a time when the dialectic between dreaming and awakening may be especially relevant and intense. Just as birth represents a dramatic ending of long pregnancy, so can treatment termination resemble the conclusion of a lengthy gestation that may be premature or full-term, yielding a new being that is healthy or handicapped. This birthing process can constitute a crisis composed, as the ancient Chinese said, of danger and opportunity. In this regard, Perdu's dream can be seen as an example of a life crisis dream (Akeret, 2019). Working long and intensively with this material in relation to the transference and Perdu's relational past awakened powerful affects and productive realizations.

Lucidity and Lack Thereof

Perdu believed he woke up, realized he had been dreaming about being on the road to Greenwich Village, then went on to discuss his earlier dream with someone like Freud. When he actually awoke, he realized that his earlier 'awakening' had been illusory. A different or complementary hypothesis would be that his mid-dream awakening was not entirely an illusion. It could be contemplated instead as a partial awakening, a moment of increased lucidity.

Yadin (2021) described such qualities of awareness and reflection as "the inner voice in dreams." He related this phenomenon to lucid dreaming—a way of waking in a dream, but not fully. In the lucid state, we continue to dream, with awareness of being both awake and asleep. In discussing Yadin's contribution, Willock (2021) noted that lucid dreamers often prize not only being aware that they are dreaming but also being able to influence oneiric events. This latter aspect of lucidity resonates with Freud's idea of wish fulfilment being the essence of dreams.

From the perspective of partial awakening, Perdu may not have been wrong to have believed he awoke, though he did not realize that this coming into awareness was only partial. He may have been more awake than he had been, but he was not fully awake.

The term, partial awakening, captures an important aspect of what Perdu may have experienced. There are no references to this phenomenon in the vast PEP Web archive of psychoanalytic articles. In other literatures, this phrase is used to indicate states of arousal between sleep stages that may be characterized by disorientation, sleep talking, and other phenomena. Dream researchers also discuss *false awakenings,* often related to incorrectly believing that one has woken to shower, eat breakfast, begin the working day, etc. There are no references to false awakening in the PEP web archive. Dr. Mahon's article furnishes us an opportunity to explore and refine our understanding of these neglected matters.

Neuroscientist Patrick McNamara (2019) notes that transitions between REM, NREM, and waking states are virtually always partial and incomplete, leading to hybrids of REM and waking, NREM and waking, or REM with NREM. When these mixed conditions occur, we can have uncanny, weird, and bizarre experiences.

McNamara believes that when we falsely think we have woken but are, in fact, still dreaming, our brain is moving towards wakefulness and, for some reason, thinks it has arrived. He suggested that if some degree of activation of the dorsolateral prefrontal cortex is the standard physiological cue that the brain uses to think it is awake, then it is reasonable to argue that this clue can sometimes be interpreted incorrectly.

He considers, as I have above, that dreaming within a dream may be more like lucid dreaming that results from a hybrid of REM and waking states. When the dorsolateral prefrontal cortex is activated during REM, the individual gains some awareness of self and so becomes aware that he is dreaming.

False awakenings involve skipping the awareness of oneself as dreaming that characterizes lucid dreaming. Instead, the awakening process would discontinue, and the individual would carry on dreaming.

"But why dream about normal morning rituals and awake activities? We do not know the answer to this question." Contemplating McNamara's query, I would suggest those false awakenings are "dreams of convenience" (Freud, 1900). A key function of dreams, Freud (1901) emphasized, is to ensure we get sufficient restorative sleep. Dreams are "the guardians of sleep" (p. 678). Sometimes we know we must get up, but we dearly want to continue slumbering. We therefore dream that we are doing all those necessary activities of daily living, permitting us to carry on sleeping.

In the 1950s, researchers at the University of Chicago discovered rapid eye movement (REM) sleep. It was also referred to as paradoxical sleep (or para sleep) because there is such active, complex brain and experiential activity happening during what is otherwise a passive, dormant state. Inherent to the paradox of dreaming is electroencephalographic and experiential ambiguity as to whether one is asleep or awake. In dreams like Perdu's, this ambiguity is elevated significantly, providing an opportunity for reflecting on the nature of dreaming, wakefulness, and mixed states.

Our capacity to differentiate between being asleep/dreaming versus awake/thinking is not always reliable. Recently

I attended a clinical presentation where an analyst said her patient presented interesting material that was not a dream. To me, the analysand's report sounded exactly like a dream. It was replete with elements that, from a reality perspective, were improbable or impossible but, in dream mentation, would not be uncommon or out of place. When I remarked on how dream-like that material seemed, the analyst responded that she, and even her patient, as they discussed the material further, were not completely sure it had not been a dream.

We do not always know when we are awake as opposed to sleeping. Psychologists, psychiatrists, neurologists, and other scientist-practitioners have contributed enormously to the growing field of research and practice often referred to as sleep medicine. They discuss such discernment difficulties with terms like: parasomnia; paradoxical insomnia (when one thinks one had little or no sleep but observers record that this was not so); microsleep (brief bursts of sleep that happen while a person is awake—often while their eyes are open and they are sitting upright, or even performing a task, such as driving a car or truck. Parts of the brain go offline for a few seconds while the rest stays awake).

Little Hans (Freud, 1909) insisted that his "thoughts" about the plumber coming to unscrew the bathtub and, some days later, returning to remove Hans's "behind and penis," were not dreams. Children can have difficulty differentiating between dreams and reality, let alone between dreams and thoughts. A preadolescent told me he used to have a recurring dream where his father came to his bed at night and led him downstairs, then turned him over to a witch. I asked him if he told his parents about this terrifying, repetitive dream. "No. I didn't know it was a dream," he responded. Adults, too, can experience difficulties discriminating between dream and reality.

The sleep-medicine literature contains numerous examples of complex confusion when one is simultaneously awake and asleep. For example, one renowned exemplar of that discipline, Dr. Carlos Schenck, noted: "This man may not always be waking up from sleep, but may actually at times be waking up from a dream-within-a-dream. Sometimes he may simultaneously wake up from sleep, his dream, and his dream-within-a-dream. Complicated shifts in an uncertain, fluctuating realm of sleep, dreams, and weird awakenings" (2007, p. 112).

Para means beyond or outside; *somnia* means sleep. Parasomnia is, therefore, any phenomena that is related to sleep but exceeds the boundaries of its more usual forms (e.g., sleepwalking). One might think of Perdu's "awakening" as a parasomnia moment. For extended discussion of these simultaneous sleep/wake states containing many fascinating illustrations, see Willock (2018, 2022).

Mahon sees Perdu's illusory awakening and subsequent dream-within-a-dream as raising important issues for the psychology of dreaming. I agree. Sleep specialists have provided many examples of patients whose nightly brainwave patterns mix typical sleep and awake electrical activity. These neurophysiological patterns make them more prone to parasomnia. We have no reason to believe Perdu had regular, simultaneous sleep/wake moments. The question therefore arises as to what might have caused this state for him during this particular dream?

Perdu believed he awoke because he was so surprised to "realize" that Connecticut and New York City were so close. This "realization" might be a manic defense against the painful reality of separation and loss associated with termination of his analysis. Manic denial of this trauma might have been sufficiently exciting that it led to arousal—a heightening of consciousness—a minor disruption of normal sleep and dreaming balanced by a prevailing wish to preserve restorative sleep and dreaming. The alternative to this brief manic defense and the ensuing moment of lucidity (partial awakening) might have been a bad dream or nightmare in relation to the trauma Mahon identified and, consequently, more serious sleep disruption.

Having partially awoken and regained his bearings, Perdu could then settle back into his dream and proceed along the royal road he was constructing to reunite with his Freudian analyst in Greenwich Village. In this complementary interpretation, emphasis is on shifting states of consciousness and partial awakening in an ongoing sleep/dream process and less on the idea of needing to construct a psychic envelope to defensively isolate a dream-within-a-dream. This alteration in accent is not to negate Mahon's reasoning but to supplement it in what I believe to be important ways in our collective efforts to navigate the regal route toward comprehending unconscious processes. One could debate whether it is truer to the data and more useful in any particular instance to speak of partial awakening and/or dreaming within a dream. Such lively discussion between competing or complementing perspectives is integral to comparative-integrative psychoanalysis (Willock, 2007).

Later, we will delve deeper into other factors relevant to the important question of what may have caused Perdu to have the illusion of awakening in the middle of his dream.

Divining Dream Thoughts and the Interpretation(s) of Dreams and Dreaming

According to Mahon, "The dream thoughts beneath the manifest content of both segments of the dream sequence could be summarized as follows":

> The child "delivered" to the house at an "odd" hour is the wish to have a child in the primal scene. The primal crime of the first part of the dream is punished by loss of bearings, loss of home. This stirs up the reality of the actual traumatic loss in childhood, which is reversed in the representation of "a child guided me home." This reversal seems not adequate to the task; "reel switching" becomes necessary. In the "new" dream portion,

after the illusion of awakening there is confession to a bearded man who represents father and analyst (neither one bearded in reality.) "Beard" represents undoing of the wish to castrate father and analyst for "forcing" him to confess, for not having a baby with him, for not allowing him to be a permanent analytic baby, for forcing him out as termination approaches. The distance between Connecticut ("connect" as opposite to the "disconnection" of loss) and Greenwich Village is "destroyed," time space altered magically in the new "Greenwich Mean Time" of unconscious timelessness (p. 123).

The richly detailed dream, associations, reflections, and interpretations presented by Mahon implicitly invite readers to participate in "dreaming" this dream, associating to it, pondering its nature, in continuing reverie. I would like to accept this tacit invitation, extending what I have already proposed in ways that might shift the emphasis in understanding in some interesting ways.

Perdu commences his dream report: "I awake at the sound of a car pulling into the driveway of our Connecticut house. It is pitch dark, but a child is being dropped off as if our home were a nursery school." Instead of, or in addition to this child being the desired offspring of Perdu and his analyst/parent, as in Mahon's main interpretation, might this youngster reflect Perdu's feeling "dropped" by his analyst in an odd, "unexpected," untimely manner, as their termination process proceeds? This dropping off can be seen as birth and abandonment—an event and a "crime" committed under the shadow of darkness. Having been ejected from his residence in Mahon's consulting room to his actual home, henceforth Perdu will have to be the principal parent and analyst for his child self. It would hardly be surprising that he might feel challenged, lost, disoriented, and in need of help with this overwhelming project.

In addition to the day/night reversal of the usual time for dropping off a child at nursery school (but not an unusual time for birthing), and the adult/child bike rider reversal, there are other turnarounds in this dream. For example, regarding this drop-off as premature birth from psycho-analysis, there is a foetus/child switch. This newborn has advanced locomotor and cognitive functions. Its "maturity" resembles the way many nonhuman animals can stand and walk immediately after birth. If one must be prematurely born from analysis, better to emerge as child than baby. A youngster able to ride a bike is capable of achieving and sus-taining balance, having no doubt endured many falls, frights, and near misses on the developmental path of learning to master this and other means of traversing distances and accomplishing developmental challenges. Such a child has many more capacities for handling this new discontinuity than does any infant. Condensing newborn and youngster prefigures the later significant compression of distance be-tween Connecticut and Greenwich Village.

In yet another reversal, Perdu might prefer to be going into the womb (home) rather than being born into the world. Analogously, he might rather go back to his analysis as op-posed to being untimely ripped from it, returned in confu-sion to Connecticut. This dream is much about reversals, including switches between states of sleep, dreaming, and wakefulness.

With the arrival of the child, the dream scene changes slightly but significantly. "I am now outside my house but lost, trying to find my bearings." Such disorientation might well be the case after birth, especially a premature, traumatic one (Willock, 2015). Having been ejected (and/or having ejected himself) from his analysis, Perdu finds himself in a confusional state. Consider Winnicott's (1971) profound in-sights on such conditions caused by separation, initially from mother:

Trauma implies that the baby has experienced a break in life's continuity, so that primitive defenses now become organized to defend against a repetition of "unthinkable anxiety" or a return of the acute confusional state that belongs to disintegration of nascent ego structure. We must assume that the vast majority of babies never experience the x+y+z quantity of deprivation. This means that the majority of children do not carry around with them for life the knowledge from experience of having been mad. Madness here simply means a *break-up* of whatever may exist at the time of *a personal continuity of existence*. After 'recovery' from x+y+z deprivation a baby has to start again permanently deprived of the root which could provide *continuity with the personal beginning* (p. 97).

Ogden (1989) refers to such breaches in root continuity as autistic-contiguous disruption. These gaps must be repaired rapidly, by any means, realistic or phantastic.

"A child on a bicycle guides me home." As if on magical cue, Perdu's more competent, central, observing ego arrives to help resolve his frightening state of mind ("to defend against a repetition of 'unthinkable anxiety' or a return of the acute confusional state that belongs to disintegration of nascent ego structure"). This rapid rescue operation is momentarily successful but evidently does not fully restore the desired self-state in a lasting manner. A more potent intervention is felt to be needed.

Soon this additional operation arrives to accomplish the desired undoing and reversal of Perdu's separation from his analyst and the history of traumatic losses it symbolizes. "Then I walk from my house in Connecticut to Greenwich Village, which in dream geography seems no more than a hundred yards." The dream succeeds in magically denying the geographical and emotional distance that this "premature" separation from his analyst involves. Disrupted contiguity is restored.

Mahon notes that "the distance between Connecticut ('connect' as opposite to the 'disconnection' of loss) and Greenwich Village is 'destroyed,' time space altered magically in the new 'Greenwich Mean Time' of unconscious timelessness." It is also noteworthy that the final syllable in Connecticut is 'cut', a word suitable for evoking the traumatic separation of 'birth' with which Perdu is struggling. Furthermore, termination can be seen as a "Mean Time." It also confronts one with the challenge of what to do in the Meantime—between the decision to terminate and the challenging accomplishment of that goal in external, objective, Greenwich time, and in the internal world of unconscious timelessness.

"I am so surprised by the spatial novelty of Connecticut's [being] a stone's throw from Greenwich Village that I wake up, an illusion, as I will discover on actual awakening. In Greenwich Village I walk into a wood-lined office in a townhouse." Freud (1900) believed wood symbolizes mother. Wood is material (from Latin 'mater' = mother). Wood = mother/matrix/womb. Birth trauma (Reik, 1924; Aaron, 2014; Willock, 2014) is symbolically undone as Perdu re-enters a tastefully wood-paneled (womb-like) enclosure.

"A bearded man, not unlike the young Freud in the Freud-Fliess era, greets me. I start to tell him the unusual dream I've just had about being lost and how it was a child who guided me home." Perdu's agonizing separation from his analyst has been reversed, perhaps even more than undone. He has found/created an uber analyst, younger and more like the bearded, founding genius of the discipline than his actual, unbearded analyst.

Trauma and Telling

Mahon emphasized the centrality of Perdu's not having been able to discuss feelings, especially overwhelming ones, with his parents. "The father's character was dramatically revealed in a childhood memory: in bed with the father after a bad dream, the child urinated while asleep. The father, startled, reprimanded the child, creating a sense of distance between son and father that was never redressed. Years later in analysis, Perdu commented bitterly: 'The warm flow of my intimacy was lost on him.' " Nocturnal urination could reflect not only intimacy but also anxiety and aggression. These other issues may also have found little place for processing with Perdu's father.

Given the slight "parasomnia" element in Perdu's adult dream, childhood urinary incontinence in the context of another bad dream is of interest. It is a minor parasomnia, a developmentally common instance in which something akin to what Freud (1900) called "access to motility" was not securely shut down during sleep due to neurological immaturity and possibly other reasons. In contrast, in Perdu's adult dream, motility was safely contained within his dream sequence despite, or perhaps partly because of, his minor parasomnia.

Although the distance between father and son was "never redressed," it was addressed in Perdu's analysis generally, and in this dream specifically. Whereas things did not go so well after a bad dream when Perdu slept with his father, they unfolded much more happily when he brought his disorienting adult dream to a Freud-like figure. That professional was well-suited to fit Perdu's wishes to have an idealized father/analyst, and to accept a decent, helpful, flawed doctor friend (Fleiss) who resembled his real analyst, and all other human beings, who inevitably possess both strengths and weaknesses. Like Freud relying on Fleiss as confidant, Perdu might have to find a post-analytic, Fleiss-type friend when he would no longer be able to take his dreams and other concerns to Dr. Mahon. In his dream, he found this figure or at least a premonition of him.

With respect to the trauma of telling, Mahon noted that much of Perdu's analysis concerned repairing his capacity to communicate. "If the breast is the first curriculum, baby talk is the first dialogue." With this metaphor, Mahon hinted that his analysand's difficulties were of very early origin. An earlier, even more fundamental curriculum is provided in the womb. In that classwomb, the curriculum is pre-babytalk. The movement from the first to the final scene in Perdu's dream captures the transition from preverbal to verbal. The nonverbal, first act emphasizes feelings, events (Fast, 1985), and sensations (sound of a car; pitch dark). Surprising things happen (child dropped off). Perdu finds himself outside, lost, struggling to find his bearings. Between uterus and breast, he is not yet in the promised land. There are miles to go before he sleeps. Vehicles (bike) and roads are required. They soon arrive, in tolerable dosage. Blessedly, it turns out that the land of milk and honey is but "a stone's throw" away. That phrase reminds me of Freud's (1920) grandson taking control of his mother's leavings by symbolically throwing her away in the form of various objects and, eventually, a spool attached to a string. For a long time, that toddler's emphasis was on *fort* (*gone!*). Only in later play was *da* (*there!*, i.e., reunion) achieved. In much shorter dreamtime, Perdu proceeded from disorientation through *fort* ("a stone's throw") to *da* (ah).

When discussing the breast as first curriculum, Mahon noted that developmental achievement cannot be sustained without some early object constancy. I would add that acquiring object constancy is made more difficult if there are earlier disruptions to autistic-contiguity that can commence in the perinatal period. This is the realm of pre-object constancy—the domain of self-constancy, self-continuity and, when things go wrong, self-disintegration.

Like the road from Connecticut to Greenwich, the path from pre- to fuller object constancy requires sensitive dosing of distance (time between separations). If the breast does not appear in a timely manner, Freud said, one must hallucinate it. In this magical manner, the Greenwich breast became miraculously close at hand and reachable.

If mother is away for x minutes, Winnicott (1971) wrote, it is not a major problem. If she is away for x + y minutes, the distress can still be repaired if she knows how to accomplish that. If mother is absent for x + y + z minutes, the damage is (I would say "may be") irreparable. The child must institute emergency defenses. Perdu called upon his hallucinatory superpowers to bridge an otherwise unbearable chasm.

Wish Fulfillment and other Dream Functions and Processes

Mahon and Perdu put considerable emphasis on core Freudian principles (wish fulfillment, superego retaliation, defense, etc.). For example:

> If one undoes the division between the two dream parts and treats the text as a seamless document, one reading of the text could be articulated as follows: "I want a baby delivered to me in darkness, a primal-scene reversal in which I am not excluded. For this, the punishment is loss of the object or loss of the love of the object" (castration fear disavowed perhaps as "regressive" object loss screens the more oedipal punishment). "'A child guided me home' redresses this. Finally, the wish to tell all to a bearded man represents the undoing of the father's castration and a man-to-man dialogue between son and parent in which aggression and sexuality need not be denied in the new space analysis has cleared for straight talk" (p.125).

Those classical ideas were probably very useful in Perdu's analysis. Here I would like to add a complementary emphasis highlighting some other dream functions and processes. From this perspective, Perdu's 3-part dream begins with at least some important elements that are "beyond the pleasure principle" (Freud, 1920)—birth, alienation from home/womb, abandonment, and disruption of autistic-contiguity. This dream phase addresses trauma and associated repetition compulsion. This endeavor may not only be automatic (PTSD) but also actively instigated as part of a search for self-saving and mastery related to prior trauma and current triggering of those ancient wounds.

An element of wish fulfillment—assisted reunion with a not so secure home base—is introduced into this trauma-based dream. In the adult/child reversal, the child becomes father to the man (Wordsworth, *My Heart Leaps Up*). This bike-riding youngster assists with affect regulation by guiding the disoriented adult back to safety. Perdu may have imagined much might have been different if only he had had the capacity when he was a child to parent his parents (cf., Ferenczi's [1949] dream of the "wise baby"), to guide them from disorientation and danger to safety.

The dream pointed to what was needed back in the day. This relatively reality-oriented narrative of dream Part 1 could not fully contain and process Perdu's triggered traumatic past. Something additional was now necessary. More magical thinking was required to at least create an illusion of closing the traumatic gap. Home alone was too lonely. A more robust, restorative, relational residence was desired. Perdu had to rapidly and radically reduce the distance between himself and his analyst, or post-analyst friend/Fleiss. His manic want (I meant to type "wand") collapsed many miles into mere yards. This glorious defeat of the dragon of distance was so exciting that it jolted him into a semi-awake state—alert enough to realize he had been dreaming, but not awake enough to spoil his slumber.

This manic or post-manic, aware, reflective state likely enabled Perdu to experience and appreciate the marvels of imagination. In reality, he will terminate his daily visits with his analyst, but in psychic reality there need be no substantial separation. In the timelessness (and relative spacelessness) of the dreaming mind, he can reunite with his analyst who has become an evolving internal object, a resource Perdu now carries within himself as a presence potentially available at all times. This need-satisfying, increasingly constant object is being further solidified in the service of dream functions emphasized by self psychologists (e.g., Fosshage, 1983) that include restoring, preserving, and growing the self. Perdu is proceeding well on Margaret Mahler's final separation-individuation phase, namely, "on the [royal] road to object constancy."

In this 3-part sequence, Perdu proceeds from a trauma-based dream with important added elements of wish-fulfillment, to slightly (hypo)manic wish-fulfillment leavened with partial awakening and realization of the power, weirdness, and wonders of imagination, to a realistic future plan for moving along the regal road from Freud to Friend (from Freudian psychoanalyst to Fleiss). In that new or renewed companion, he will find many of the wonderful qualities facilitating and promoting dialogue that he found in Freud (academically) and in his actual analyst, Mahon.

Earlier I began addressing Mahon's important question about what stimulated Perdu's dream-within-a-dream or, as I emphasize, his partial awakening. I talked of arousal related to desperately needed manic defense. Most or all psychic functions can be used for either self-protective or growth-facilitating purposes. With respect to the latter, Perdu's mania might be regarded as introducing a necessary element of stimulating magic realism into his narrative—a respectable literary device. The road to Greenwich is many miles long but one can, via the power of imagination, reduce it to a short distance that can be easily traversed. In psychic reality, one can access the inaccessible. Initially there may be some manic defense at work, but partial awakening transforms defense into adaptation, contributing to revelation and wisdom.

In the title of an important article, Grotstein (1970) raised the crucial question: *Who is the dreamer who dreams the dream and who is the dreamer who understands it?* Elaborating on Grotstein's and McDougall's (1985) ideas on how dreams require set designers, choreographers, scriptwriters, location scouts, costume designers, actors, and many other talents, I described this assemblage of subselves as the Dream Team (Willock, 2021). This intelligent, competent, coordinated group has a receptive audience in mind, namely the dreamer who watches and understands the play in which he has also been recruited to be usually the main, and also the auxiliary actors.

"Every dream has an *arousing* effect" (Freud, 1900, p. 575). The self that observes the dream and derives benefit from it may sometimes need to be even more "wide awake" than usual in order to fully register and ponder the importance of the play s/he is watching. This necessary arousal may require the illusion of actually being awake to help not only grasp the dream and contemplate it but also to preserve it in memory for future exploration with one's analyst, friend, or self—in keeping with Khan's (1962) definition of the "good dream."

Mahon underscored that the dream-within-a-dream treatment of Perdu's childhood trauma that had been so much explored, now seemed to generate new affects, and more intense memory. It may have been more the partial awakening, rather than a dream-within-a-dream, that promoted these new feelings, intensified memory, and therapeutic benefit.

"Mr. P was puzzled that the reality of being lost as a child, which had received much scrutiny in the analysis, could still show up in a dream-within-a-dream, as if to insist that it still needed to be disavowed intensely!" This perplexity and frustration aligned with the analytic dyad's focus on the idea that dreams within dreams mean that something especially painful is being doubly distanced. From the perspective of partial awakening, the reappearance of this material was not so much indicative of it having to be intensely disavowed (though that is true) but rather to signal that it needed to be faced and worked with some more and that this could be usefully accomplished or commenced in a dream assisted and fortified by partial awakening.

This difference in viewpoint concerning partial awakening versus dream-within-dream mirrors the sometimes vociferous debate in the literature as to whether dreams mainly conceal or reveal. Protagonists have at times preferred extreme polar positions. Comparative-integrative psychoanalysis, aimed at separating the wheat from the chaff in all positions, and exploring to what extent a both/and rather than an either/or perspective might be viable, would suggest that neither polarized assertion may be comprehensively true. Both concealment and revelation can manifest in any dream and in any dream element.

À la Recherche du Temps Perdu (In Search of Lost Time)

In naming his analysand Mr. Perdu, Mahon may have wanted to underscore the central importance of loss in Perdu's life and psyche. I imagine he might have thought of this French word in relation to its prominence in the famous title of Marcel Proust's masterpiece, *À la Recherche du Temps Perdu*. It is not only time, but also opportunities that are lost—the what might have beens but only for what failed to happen, or happened instead. Perdu's dream demonstrates that these losses can be revisited and a process of reparation can be commenced in dreams and, later, be continued in waking life. This beneficial transition from dreaming to waking life may be facilitated by dreaming one is awake.

Thissearchforlosttime(andlostrelationships,experiences,and opportunities) can be another important function of dreaming. Like the unbidden memories that came to Proust, dreams are a venue in which consciously unbidden experiences arise for our contemplation, processing, and potential benefit. An alternative name for Mr. Perdu could be Monsieur Recherche (Mr. Research, Mr. Searcher). This moniker would put the emphasis on Perdu's creative response to the trauma of loss rather than on his retraumatization.

Khan's (1962) "good dream" incorporates an unconscious wish that enables sleep to be sustained and, upon awakening, is available for processing. When early satisfactions have been unreliable, the capacity to use "mnemic images of satisfaction" (Khan, p.28) to mobilize dream-wishes is lacking or distorted. In contrast, a good dream indicates "a psychic capacity … the dream increment of ego-strength" (p. 25) on which analytic work depends. When this function is disturbed by ego-distortions, primitive defenses, or psychotic anxieties, one tends to act out in harmful ways. In Perdu's dream, he demonstrates his evolving capacity to mobilize wishes to self-right (Lichtenberg, Lachmann, & Fosshage, 2011) in the face of disorienting separation. Rather than having to actually awaken to process this dream, he is felicitously able to bring it to an internalized analyst while still sleeping. Later, he can continue processing this remarkable phantasy during the daytime with his wife, real analyst, and perhaps others (e.g., a Fleiss-like friend).

When I ponder what Perdu has lost and seeks, his nocturnal reverie brings to me, unbidden, John Denver's beautiful song, *Take Me Home, Country Roads*. Perdu might sing: "Take me home, Connecticut Roads. Take me home to the place I belong." His psychic residence is becoming a relational matrix where he feels increasingly at home. It combines Connecticut/ Greenwich Village/Johannesburg, past/present/future, and being lost/found/revitalized.

Comparative-Integrative Psychoanalysis

In my effort to participate in Perdu's dream, Jung's (1974) ideas about subjective and objective levels of interpretation were valuable background concepts. Mahon mostly saw the child as a dropped-off baby that Perdu conceived/wished to bear in a primal scene derivative with his analyst. In contrast, on Jung's subjective level, that child would not be an object, but rather a subject, namely Perdu himself, being abandoned.

The competent, bike-riding youngster could also be Ferenczi's (1923) "wise baby." While an adult Perdu floundered, this young one, sage and talented beyond his years, could easily understand what was needed to save the day. A sapient part of himself like this could help contain Perdu's anxieties as he approached his post-analytic, self-analysis.

There are limits to the wisdom and power of infants. The reality of these shortcomings must sometimes be buttressed by manic magic. Klein (1935, 1940) originally referred to this omnipotent stance as the Manic Position, designed to defend against Depressive anxieties like separation, dependency, vulnerability, and loss. From a neo-Kleinian perspective, I would add that mania can be called upon to transcend, or at least provide a wild, comforting illusion or delusion of overcoming the earliest anxieties of the Autistic-Contiguous Position.

Jung anticipated Kohut's self-state dreams, seeing these nocturnal hallucinations as "spontaneous self-portrayal in symbolical form of the actual situation in the unconscious" (Jung, 1916, p.263). In the British Object Relational tradition, Fairbairn pushed beyond this useful snapshot or x-ray perspective in his idea of dreams as struggles to not only depict but also to work through and progress beyond object relational dilemmas. Perdu's dream provides a fine illustration of a dreamer doing just that.

The prospective function of dreams (Jung, 1916) involves an unconscious, anticipatory, guiding function pointing consciousness toward a better path. This purposive function differs from Freud's idea of the unconscious as a repository of unacceptable, repressed infantile wishes seeking covert gratification. Jung's unconscious is an autonomous, intelligent, creative agent, selecting apt images for developmental purposes. From this perspective, Perdu's dream may be serving to guide him toward further actualizing his imaginative and self-analytic functions, and turning to others for intimate dialogue, promoting object constancy, continuing resolution of old trauma, and growth.

Kleinian analyst Hanna Segal (2018) described predictive dreams that are designed to expel beta elements (Bion, 1962) rather than processing and benefiting from them. Events from a predictive dream are soon enacted in one's analysis with the aim of dumping, rather than exploring them. Purdu's dream could be seen as a predictive one that foreshadowed sharing it with his analyst in waking life that was healthily aimed not at expulsion but at growth-oriented investigation.

Self-psychologist Marian Tolpin (2002) emphasized the co-existence of trailing and leading edges in dreams and other psychic phenomena. Perdu provides a good illustration of these opposite thrusts. Early on, his dream grapples with a trailing edge—processing separation from his analyst via images that evoke past separation trauma. He adds increasing amounts of wish fulfillment, proceeding from relatively simple, symbolic forms of that to slightly more manic versions. At that point, he puts on his psychic brakes, shaking himself into a partially awake state, to reflect on his experience and process it. Having effected that settling, grounding function, achieving a contemplative position, he proceeds to the leading edge of his dream, envisioning beneficial post-analytic relationships and productive dialogue with his internal analyst.

These brief references to Jung, Klein, British Object Relations, Self Psychology, and a neoKleinian framework (Ogden) illustrate the value of a comparative-integrative approach to psychoanalysis. Any or all of these approaches, and others (e.g., Interpersonal and Relational psychoanalysis) are valuable in themselves. We massively augment the utility of single approaches when we are open to engaging with the multiple perspectives available to us.

Oedipal Defense Against Earlier Anxieties?

Whereas Mahon emphasized oedipal wishes, resulting superego punishment, and defenses, I pondered Perdu's possibly more primary preoccupation with earlier issues concerning separation. Might comparative-integrative psychoanalysis envision more than additive validity to these perspectives?

Fairbairn (1944), then Guntrip (1969) regarded neuroses as defenses against earlier schizoid anxieties. This may not be as universally true as they believed, but it can sometimes be the case. Kohut later articulated a related idea, namely, that oedipal pathology only arises when there is pre-existing self/selfobject pathology. From these viewpoints, Mahon's interpretation that Perdu wanted to conceive a baby with his analyst/parents, could be seen as manic denial of categorical differences (boundaries), in this instance between sexes and generations. In this worldview in which anything is possible, there are no frustrating separations, distances, impossibilities. Despite being a child, and male, he can conceive a baby with his parents. Here he has conveniently obliterated the first phase of Mahler's separation-individuation journey—differentiation. Symbiotic undifferentiation (dedifferentiation) prevails, when needed. Greenwich Mean Time succumbs to timespacelessness.

Mahon wrote that Perdu's reading of Freud was deep and well integrated into his overall philosophical knowledge, and was a factor that could serve as resistance at times. It seems Perdu could draw on the intricacies of oedipal theory, not only for creative enlightenment, but also to defend against more fundamental anxieties stimulated by termination.

Ockham's Blade

Occam's Razor is a principle of theory construction or evaluation according to which, other things being equal, explanations that posit fewer entities, or fewer kinds of entities, are preferred to explanations that posit more entities and assumptions. In laypersons' terms, the most economical (simple) theory is often best.

Following that guiding heuristic, named after a misspelling of William of Ockham, a brilliant medieval philosopher, logician, and theologian, the idea of partial awakening in Perdu's dream might be more economical than more complicated, perhaps confusing, contemplation of dreams within dreams, leading to questions as to which dream is within which dream, and so forth.

Rather than Perdu's dream being mostly about the need to sequester traumatic recollections that refuse to go away, one might emphasize more his desire to comprehend current stress on its own terms, and in relation to past trauma, for the purpose of growth rather than simply survival.

If one had to choose between sources of anxiety, the first step in Freud's (1926) famous anxiety series (loss of the object) might be in some ways even more important (foundational) than subsequent phallic-oedipal issues (loss of part of the body, etc.). Contemporary triggers and adaptive context (Langs, 1973) challenges might sometimes be even more important, or more productively explored, than related past trauma. Comparative-integrative analysis by multiple psychoanalysts might profitably consider how these multiple factors and viewpoints challenge and enrich our evolving understanding of this fascinating material.

Given that Professor Perdu reads at least classical psychoanalysis (Freud), he might encounter this article. If so, some ideas in it might stimulate productive dialogue between him and his now internalized, evolving analyst (Mahon/Freud).

Might these Ideas help Comprehend other Dreams within Dreams?

Berman's (1985) patient shared the following dream(s):

> I'm in bed with J (her boyfriend). He's caressing my vagina and it feels very exciting. Then I feel another hand there; I think it belongs to M (her son). I wake up, terrified, and I'm in the bedroom with J. I demand to know if that was M's hand. He answers evasively. Then M walks into the bedroom and I scream at him to get out (p. 75).

In her associations, this patient referred to her inner and outer dreams. (Readers might be interested in knowing whether these terms were common parlance in this analytic dyad, or relatively unprecedented.) The inner dream painfully recalled interpretations Berman had made about her seductive behaviour toward her son: how shocked and guilty it made her feel to consider having sexual feelings toward him, and how angry she felt at Berman for pointing it out. The outer dream reminded her of a family party she attended the night before with her boyfriend and her son. She had become a little drunk and was sitting on her boyfriend's lap while her son watched TV in the next room. She teasingly told her boyfriend that she could never understand what he and her son found so exciting about watching football on television. In the process of telling him this she slipped and called him by the name of a former boyfriend and was concerned that this would make him jealous.

Berman interpreted her dream in the form of a reconstruction: that it expressed her feelings as a child "outside" her parent's bedroom, filled with excitement and jealousy, and wishing to participate on the "inside." He further suggested that her anger with her son reflected her parents' attitude toward her childhood sexual curiosity that had become incorporated as her own attitude.

The patient was able to accept this interpretation with less defensiveness and more thoughtful reflection than before. In subsequent sessions, she produced further associations to the dream. The other hand caressing her vagina reminded her of masturbating as a child; feeling guilty, and fearing that mother would detect the offensive odour on her fingers. The analytic couple linked this with the observational quality of her adolescent and adult fantasies, postulating that her childhood masturbation served to discharge primal scene excitement.

Rather than understanding Berman's patient having an outer and an inner dream, I would see her *one* dream as having begun as a wish-fulfilling (sexual) dream. It then touched upon a traumatic area (incest), analogous to Mahon's description of his patient having contacted past/continuing trauma in his dream. This traumatic activation pushed Berman's patient 'beyond the pleasure principle' (Freud, 1923). That is, rather than continuing in keeping with Freud's first theory of dreaming (wish fulfillment), the dreamwork shifted to dealing with overwhelming experience (impingement) in keeping Freud's second theory of dreaming (trauma mastery).

The possibility of her son stroking her genitals shocked Berman's patient into a hyperalert state. Having touched trauma, she 'wakes'. 'Waking' reduces the frightening intensity of the previous experience: she realizes it was just a dream. She may now be a bit more awake, including neurophysiologically, but she is still dreaming. As in parasomnia, she may be simultaneously awake and asleep/dreaming, with the accent on the latter state. She has 'woken' into a continuing dream. 'Weird awakenings' indeed, as Schenck (and McNamara) described these incomplete state shifts.

This dream change differs significantly from nightmares from which we are usually jolted wide awake, thanks to Freud's (1900) 'night watchman' who extricates us from what he has determined is too much overwhelming material for us to go on dreaming. This patient's nocturnal protector is more nuanced and sophisticated than Freud may have imagined. Hiss sensitivity and talents go beyond what Freud discussed. He allows Berman's patient to obtain the relief of *feeling* she has woken up from just a dream *and* to continue obtaining necessary restorative sleep, and further dream the disturbing material. The skill of this nocturnal guardian helps us develop Freud's night watchman concept in interesting, useful ways.

This patient's experience could be seen as a dream within a dream. Alternatively, it could be viewed simply as a continuation of the original dream in a slightly (necessarily) adaptively altered state of consciousness. These descriptions of these processes might be viewed as complementary. Dream within a dream has an appealing, poetic quality. My description may be more precise and provide a better, fuller description of what may be happening, and why (the adaptive functions of these dream/sleep processes).

Commenting on Berman's patient's dream, Balter (2006)

wrote: "This dream depicts a nested dream *in statu na-scendi*. The dream work made the initial (sexual) events in the containing dream retrospectively into a nested dream" (p.668). Rather than accenting this dream having been transformed after the fact into a dream-within-a-dream, I would be inclined to regard the original dream as continuing, not seamlessly, in a new key. Rather than one part of the dream *containing* the other part, they are simply sequential. Both parts of the dream are contained in a single phase of REM sleep. There might be some very minor alteration in an electroencephalographic recording of that dream period indicating brief, slight, partial awakening in the context of that REM dreaming.

Silber's patient (1983) reported the following dream:

> I go to group therapy and David B. is the therapist. He looks stronger than he does in real life. I feel anxious about revealing my feelings in the group. I want to talk about the dream I'd had that night—in the dream *David's wife, Martha, tickled me.* Then I begin to get feelings about this therapy being second best because it is in a group and not one to one.

This dream took place while the patient was struggling with feelings about being part of a church discussion group led by David B.

Like Mahon's example, Silber's dream emerged in the final phase of the analysis. Could it be that such dreams might be more likely to arise during that stage, perhaps because analysands are grappling with the challenge of henceforth needing to bring dreams and other material to someone other than their analyst? Silber's patient feared she would be discussing her dream with a practitioner of what she viewed as a second-rate modality, group therapy. On the other hand, she "upgraded" him from being leader of a discussion group to being her group therapist, someone at home and in the role of emotional helper. As part of this elevation, she noted that he looked "stronger than he does in real life." In contrast, Mahon's analysand envisaged *unambivalent* upgrade—all the way to young Freud himself. Both patients were struggling with whether their post-analytic confidants and internal analysts would be better or worse than the analysts they were losing.

I would like to know whether Silber's analysand actually had the dream about David's wife tickling her. If so, was it immediately before the group therapy dream? Did she wake up in actuality, or phantasy, and remember the dream before falling back to sleep to continue it? In any case, there is at least a sort of dream-within-a-dream here, even if we do not know if and when it may have actually occurred. These are important details.

Harris (2002) reports that an artist, G, told her that after the murderous assault on the World Trade Center, her patient's child appeared one morning to tell her:

> that in her dream she woke up and went to the window and another building was falling. There are dreams within dreams in which this child reports conviction and knowledge. G thinks of the dream as a wish to join her parents in what they jointly know, what binds them as a family with this new shared history (p. 465).

Harris referred to this child's convincing dreams within dreams. It would be interesting to know more about this youngster's history of such dreams. In this particular instance, I would tend to accent this as a child reporting to her mother a frightening dream, and minimize the dream-within-in-a-dream aspect, as Harris seems to have done. The child's mother reacted to it as a dream (not emphasizing a dream nested in another dream). It would, of course, be interesting to know what the dream had been prior to this child 'waking' up, then going to the window to observe another building falling. In the meantime, I would be inclined to see this as a single dream that switched into a new key, featuring a feeling of being awake, much like Berman's (and Mahon's) patient's dream. Given that this dream related to the murdering of multitudes in the 9/11 attack on New York City's World Trade Center, one can imagine the nightwatchman deciding G's daughter must not continue relaxedly asleep but, rather, must be 'awake' and observing the catastrophe from a distance rather than being passively lying down and perhaps at the very heart of the disaster. This girl was able to continue obtaining the sleep she needed and was 'awake' enough to be relatively safe and able to recall the dream in the morning and bring it to her mother for further alphabetizing.

Mahon summarized the sparse literature on dreams within dreams by remarking that it rarely went beyond what Freud had to say on this matter in *The Interpretation of Dreams*. Freud devoted a mere paragraph to this topic. In decades of subsequent writing, he never said anything further about this matter. More precision in our depictions of dreams within dreams and greater conceptual rigor, and provision of contextual detail, would be highly desirable for creating a cumulative body of investigation concerning this captivating subject.

Are Dreams Still the *Via Regia* for Understanding Unconscious Processes?

Dreams offer us a valuable *third* that patients and analysts can contemplate together. At other times, we attend to analysands' reports of their experience and may sometimes find ourselves in difficult transference/countertransference experiences or enactments that can be challenging, for one or both parties, to regard with optimal objectivity. Patients may accuse us of having done something bad, or failing to do something good. In either case, charged ambiences can make it difficult to preserve a more contemplative, rational, dialogic atmosphere. In contrast, working with patients' dreams can be more like discussing and associating to works of art, like paintings, poems, or films. Analyst and analysand can enjoy trying to understand peculiarities and unrealistic features in dreams, combining multiple insights, cherishing what light these discernments can throw on important psychic operations.

Hopefully what I have written illustrates how useful and fascinating I find dreams as therapeutic and research tools. They provide an extremely interesting, powerful path to understanding unconscious processes. There are other routes, such as parapraxes, humor, transference, countertransference, enactments, symptoms, and projective instruments like the Rorschach and Thematic Apperception Test. Dreams do, however, have one advantage: they are familiar and fascinating to most people. For many analysts, these nocturnal hallucinations are the regal route; others might vote for different paths.

I tend to concur with those who regard *The Interpretation of Dreams* (Freud, 1900) as the most important book ever penned in psychology. It is not the last word on this subject, but it launched a multitude of marvelous projects pertaining not only to nocturnal mentation but also to so much more (e.g., understanding symptoms, psychosis, perversion, character formation, creativity, and thought itself). It introduced us to a royal road that has enabled us to visit, comprehend, and explore many fascinating domains that have been crucial in the evolution of human thought. Freud's profound insights that he shared in his classic text continue to assist us mightily in these necessary investigations.

From ancient Greek roots, we derived the word diagnosis, meaning to know through dividing and distinguishing. Approaching Professor Perdu's dream from multiple perspectives permitted us to divine different facets of its nature. We came to know not only his dream but also his condition and its challenges more fully. Looking at this clinical specimen as a dream-within-a-dream leads one in certain directions as one accommodates to and challenges existing theory. Regarding it more in terms of partial awakenings takes one to different possibilities. Our diagnoses, that is, our differentiated understanding of dreams and dreamers, are enriched by these multiple approaches that can challenge, complement, and enrich each other in our quest for ever better comprehension.

References

Akeret, R. (2019). The escape from alligator mom. In: Willock, B., Curtis, R.C., & Sapountzis, I. (Eds.), *Psychoanalytic Perspectives on Knowing and Being Known: In Theory and Clinical Practice.* New York & Oxon: Routledge, pp. 22–27.

Balter, L. (2005). Nested ideation and the problem of reality. *Psychoanal. Q.,* 74(3):661–701.

Berman, L.E. (1985). Primal scene significance of a dream-within-a-dream. *Int. J. Psycho-Anal.,* 66:75–76.

Bion, W.R. (1962). The psychoanalytic theory of thinking II. A theory of thinking. *International Journal of Psycho-Analysi*s, 43:306–310.

Fairbairn, W.R.D. (1944). *Psychoanalytic Studies of the Personality.* London: Tavistock.

Fast, I. (1985). *Event Theory: A Piaget-Freud Integration.* Hillsdale, N.J.: Lawrence Erlbaum.

Ferenczi, S. (1923). Der traum vom "gelehrten Säugling." [The dream of the "wise baby."] Internationale Zeitschrift fürärztliche Psychoanalyse, IX:70.

——— (1949). Confusion of tongues between adults and the child—The language of tenderness and of passion. *Int. J. Psycho-Anal.,* 30:225–230.

Fosshage, J.L. (1983). The psychological function of dreams: A revised psychoanalytic perspective. In, Melvin R. Lansky (ed.), *Essential Papers on Dreams.* New York: New York University Press, pp. 249–271.

Freud, S. (1900). The interpretation of dreams. *Standard Edition, 4, 5*.

——— (1901). On dreams. *Standard Edition*, 5:629–686.

——— (1909). Analysis of a phobia in a five-year-old boy. *Standard Edition 10*:3–152.

——— (1920). Beyond the pleasure principle. *Standard Edition, 18*.

——— (1926). Inhibitions, symptoms and anxiety. *Standard Edition 20*:75–176.

Green, C. (1968). *Lucid Dreams*. London: Hamish Hamilton.

Grotstein, J.S. (1979). Who is the dreamer who dreams the dream and who is the dreamer who understands It—A Psychoanalytic inquiry into the ultimate nature of being. *Contemp. Psychoanal.*, 15:110–169.

Guntrip, H. (1969). *Schizoid Phenomena, Object-Relations and the Self*. New York: International Universities Press.

Harris, A. (2002). Dialogues and monologues. *Psychoanal. Dial.*, 12(3):457–472.

Jung, C. (1916). General aspects of dream psychology. In: *Collected Works, 8*. Princeton, NJ: Princeton University Press, 1969, pp. 237–280.

Khan, M.R.M. (1962). Dream psychology and the evolution of the psychoanalytic situation. *Int. J. Psycho-Anal.*, 43:21–31.

Klein, M. (1935). A contribution to the psychogenesis of manic-depressive states. *The Writings of Melanie Klein, 1*. London: Hogarth.

——— (1940). Mourning and its relation to manic-depressive states. *The Writings of Melanie Klein, 1*. London: Hogarth.

Langs, R. (1973). *The technique of psychoanalytic psychotherapy.* New York: Aronson.

Lichtenberg, J., Lachmann, F., & Fosshage, J. (2011), *Psychoanalysis and Motivational Systems: A New Look.* New York: Routledge.

Mahon, E.J. (2002). Dreams within dreams. *Psychoanalytic Study of the Child,* 57:118–130.

McDougall, J. (1985). *Theaters of the mind: illusion and truth on the psychoanalytic stage.* New York: Basic Books.

McNamara, P. (2019). A dream-within-a-dream. *Psychology Today,* Sept. 26. https://www.psychologytoday.com/ca/blog/dream-catcher/201909/dream-within-dream.

Ogden, T.H. (1989). On the concept of an autistic-contiguous position. *Int. J. Psycho-Anal.,* 70:127–140.

Rank, O. (1924). *The trauma of birth.* New York: Harper & Row.

Schenck, C.H. (2007). *Sleep: A Groundbreaking Guide to the Mysteries, the Problems, and the Solutions.* NY: Penguin.

Segal, H. (2018). The function of dreams. In: J.S. Grotstein, (Ed), *Do I Dare Disturb the Universe? A Tribute to W.R. Bion,* pp.579–588. Oxon & New York: Routledge.

Silber, A. (1983). A significant dream-within-a-dream. *J. Amer. Psychoanal. Assn.* 31:899–915.

Tolpin, A. (2002). Doing psychoanalysis of normal development: Forward edge transferences. *Progress in Self Psychology.* A. Goldberg (Ed.). Hillsdale, NJ: The Analytic Press, pp.167–190.

Willock, B. (2007). *Comparative-Integrative Psychoanalysis.* Hillsdale, NJ: The Analytic Press.

———— (2014). The mutually facilitating maturational matrix. *Psychoanalytic Dialogues*, 24:364–373.

———(2015). Psychoanalysis of prematurity. *Psychoanalytic Dialogues*, 25: 34–49.

———— (2017). Dreams and self rebirthing. *Psychoanalytic Dialogues,* 27(3):264–277.

———— (2018). *The Wrongful Conviction of Oscar Pistorius: Science Transforms our Comprehension of Reeva Steenkamp's Shocking Death.* Durham, NC: Torchflame Books.

———— (2021). Multiple selves and the nature of dreaming. *Psychoanal. Dial.,* 31(2):234–246.

_____ (2022). On dreaming, parasomnia, dream enactment, and murder. *Psychoanalytic Psychology,* 39(2): 97–110.

Winnicott, D.W. (1971). *Playing and Reality.* New York: Penguin Books.

Yadin, Z.S. (2021). The inner voice in dreams. *Psychoanal. Dial.,* 31(2):219–233.

Dreams and the Wish for Immortality

Arnold D. Richards

Hold fast to dreams, for if dreams die
life is a broken-winged bird that cannot fly.

–Langston Hughes

This paper proposes that wishes for longevity and immortality should be added to Freud's list of wish fulfillment (sexual and aggressive) in dreams. The author provides examples of his own dreams to support his thesis. The paper also maintains that the distinction between wish fulfillment and traumatic dreams is not as absolute as Freud maintains; so that traumatic dreams may also be wish-fulfilling. The paper discusses how the child's knowledge of death develops from early life on. The fear of immortality, as well as the wish for immortality, is considered.

Wishes for immortality and longevity are among the most universal of human desires. A wealth of cultural and historical evidence supports this observation. Ancient civilizations preserved bodies, built tombs and pyramids to house them, and provided all the necessities for an afterlife. Immortality, life after death, and resurrection are essential aspects of many primitive and modern religions. Yet in *The Interpretation of Dreams,* Freud's landmark study of wishes and how we represent them to ourselves, this fundamental wish is not addressed.

Freud's revolutionary discovery was that dreams are not about predicting the future or remembering the past; they are about desire—the basic wishes foundational to our personhood—and its dangers. He maintained explicitly that "in the unconscious every one of us is convinced of his own immortality." (Freud, 1915. p. 288). And he certainly had profound wishes of his own about living forever. He believed that *The Interpretation of Dreams* would assure his immortality (Fliess letters, 1904)—and it probably has. Yet in it, by focusing exclusively on wishes about sexuality and aggression at the expense of wishes about life and death, he acted out his own hallmark thesis—that in our attempts to fulfill forbidden wishes we disguise them from ourselves. He omitted from his inventory of conflicted longings the consoling wish for immortality in the face of the absolute primacy of death.

I will not engage here with the metapsychological assertions Freud advanced in the dream book, which have engaged psychoanalysts for more than a century now: the principle of psychic determinism; the existence of an unconscious; the distinction between manifest and latent content; the sleep-preserving function of dreams, and so on. My intention is only to demonstrate that in what was perhaps his most enduring and influential work, Freud left out the ur-wish of the human animal. In so doing, he established an absence that simultaneously enshrines and denies the importance of death in our psychic lives, and with it the compensatory wish to escape it. His book is a manifestation of the dynamic paradox that the more we desire immortality, the more dangerous it is to confront that desire, despite his *bon mots* on the subject ("the goal of all life is Death" [Freud, 1920, p., 39]). Let me make two general points at the outset. In Freud's view there were two kinds of dreams. The central proposition in *The Interpretation of Dreams* is that dreams are wish fulfillments, specifically of childhood sexual and aggressive wishes. He sees in a dream about strawberries a child's wish for epicurean sensual delight. But most of the childhood sexual and aggressive wishes that Freud had in mind had to do with the universal ambivalences of the Oedipus complex. It was not until two decades had passed that he identified a second category of dreams, those representing traumatic events. He considered these an exception to the rule of dream as wish fulfillment (Freud, 1900). I will show that many immortality dreams blur the distinction between wish-fulfillment dreams and trauma dreams that Freud considered absolute. This is another reason to study these dreams.

Second, Freud's belief that some dreams are "beyond the pleasure principle" supported his argument for a death instinct: the recognition of the universal truth that organic matter ultimately becomes inorganic matter, and that there is a push for the cessation of stimulation (the *nirvana principle,* which Freud borrowed from Barbara Low (Freud, 1920, p. 55).

As I have said, however, I believe that wishes for longevity and immortality, and the fears that go with them, also demand— and threaten—fulfillment, and that therefore the wish-fulfillment category of dreams is motivated by a life instinct. For if dreams are imaginary compensations for unsatisfied desires, how can we recognize only desires for sexual and aggressive satisfaction? This makes for a very narrow view of human motivation, a critique that has often been offered of Freud's view of the human personality (Kardiner, Karush, and Oversey, 1959).

I have argued that psychoanalysis is at root the science of motivation (Richards, 1996). But it is hard to understand the vast range of human experience without a broader perspective on the wishes that motivate us, and these wishes surely include—we can see them in Freud himself—the desire to cheat death, to live forever, or at least for a very long time. Without them how can we understand our enduring

105

concerns with legacy, with political engagement, with art, literature, and other creative activities? Every creator creates for an audience—the one that is present now and, perhaps even more important, the one that will be there in the future.

Like Freud, I was alerted to these considerations by my own dreams. And this brings up a stipulation: Freud indicated in *The Interpretation of Dreams* that he suppressed some of his interpretations out of consideration for the privacy of others. Other people's privacy is not an issue in this paper. I have some concerns about my own privacy, of course, but I have been careful not to withhold any associations affecting the propositions that I offer. This is in contradistinction to Freud, who told Jung on the boat to New York that he had also limited *self*-revelation on the grounds that his authority would suffer if he said too much about his own dreams. I am not worried about my own authority, but I do suggest that to engage publicly with his immortality wishes might have required from Freud a confrontation with himself that he did not relish.

The night before I was to give a lecture on dream theory in Wuhan, China, I had the dream that awakened my first awareness of the importance of the wish for immortality, and its dynamics in dreams. In the dream a salesman was selling me a pen that he said had been invented by his grandmother. It had four sealed cartridges, each of which could write for two and a half years.

One piece of the day residue was a conversation at dinner that evening with my wife and the Chinese director of the program where I was speaking. We were talking about how we wrote papers. My wife said that she writes all of her papers on the computer; I said I write mine in longhand, and have them transcribed; I use a pen. Another residuum of "real life" was that I had been bothered for several days by a fight I was having with my institute. I was being constantly thwarted in my wishes to participate in certain activities, and I was very frustrated. I thought to myself, "At some point in the future I will write a lot about all of this. The power of the pen!"

That thought gave rise to another one: that I was now as old as Freud was when he died. I was hoping to live at least ten years more, and to write many more papers. The grandmother in the dream I associated to my own grandmother, whose loss when I was five was my first encounter with death. In the dream, however, the salesman's grandmother was still alive. I could also identify oedipal wishes related to my father and my analyst, but you have all heard hundreds of thousands of such already, and anyway they aren't relevant here.

After this I began paying close attention to representations of death, immortality, and longevity in my dreams. Many of us have had dreams, or even a series of them, in which dead persons aren't dead. For about a week after a close friend died, I had dreams in which he was alive—as alive as can be. I knew he was dead, but in the dream his death was negated—my friend himself did not seem to know about it. Here is one example of Freud's two categories of dreams overlapping. In one sense this was a trauma dream; it felt like one, and my friend's death, and his dying, were certainly traumatic for me as well as for him. But the dream negated the trauma, and represented and fulfilled my wish that it had never happened and that my friend was still among us. And I will not deny that a dream about a dead person being alive may also have to do with the negation of the dreamer's aggressive wishes toward that person—with guilt—or with his own wish for immortality. Human motivations are complex, and cannot always be strictly separated.

Once I was paying attention, examples piled up quickly. I had a set of recurrent dreams of a close colleague, friend, and mentor: Martin Bergmann, who died two years ago at the age of 101. In one of these he was standing next to Yosef Yerushalmi, whom I knew less well but admired a lot—a historian who had written about Jewish history and also about Freud's *Moses and Monotheism*. In the

107

dream, he and Bergmann were standing next to each other, and I heard myself say or think, "They are standing tall." The day residue in that case was that the new director of an organization I am connected with had told me that Yerushalmi had been his mentor at Columbia University.

In a more recent dream, I am at a movie theater, sitting in the loge. On the other side of the theater are Martin Bergmann and his wife Ridi, who is still alive at 98. Martin, who is dead, is represented as alive in the dream. In the second part of the dream, I have returned to the same theater, and sitting in the row behind me is Ridi Bergmann with some other people. I see her face and I think to myself, "Her skin is not wrinkled. Even though she is old, she looks young."

I believe that dreams like these represent wishes for longevity and/or immortality, sometimes for ourselves, and sometimes for others—the wish not to die oneself, and the wish for the people one loves not to die. Both altruism and selfishness come into play here. But why do we dream these things instead of just thinking about them? Why, according to Freud's understanding of the mechanics and purpose of dreams, must they be relegated to the unconscious? Why are they forbidden? What is the fear? I suggest that in longevity and immortality dreams the threat is something far more powerful than a vengeful father or even the inexorability of death. As I will show, it is the recognition that, wishes notwithstanding, immortality is the greatest terror of them all.

Freud wrote that "The child's idea of being dead has nothing in common with ours, apart from the word. Children know nothing of the horrors of corruption, of the freezing ice cold grave, of terrors, of eternal nothingness—ideas which grown-up people find it so hard to tolerate, as is proven by the myths of future life." He told of an intelligent boy of twelve who remarked after the sudden death of his father, "I know father is dead but what I can't understand is why he doesn't come for supper" (Freud, 1900, p. 254. n.1). We can smile at this, and it is certainly true that our understanding of death becomes more sophisticated as we mature cognitively and psychologically. But it is important to recognize that our understanding is always, and will always be, profoundly incomplete. More about this later.

Since Freud didn't delineate the way children's death ideas develop, let me offer a framework. It can take up to twelve before children understand the key components of death—universality, irreversibility; functionality; and causality—but many children achieve a reasonably mature understanding by the age of seven or so, at least intellectually (which is as far as any of us get). Their comprehension grows and matures as they do, but it takes a while before they can encompass the whole of this intimidating concept. Young children may undergo catastrophic separations, but they do not necessarily equate these with the experience of death or even of bereavement. Toddlers have grasped enough to worry about death and perhaps to threaten with it—"If you do that you'll die; If you do that I'll kill you"—but death has little abstract reality to them. For many children the closest available analog to death is sleep, which can cause problems itself.

Furthermore, studies show that young children harbor a dual view of death in which the body may die, but the mind is still alive.. A vignette reported by K.R. Olson in *Psychology Today* (Olson, 2013) depicts this developmental dualism. A four-year-old has just learned that a neighboring cat has died.

The mother asks: "Can he still move?"

The four-year-old answers: "No."

Mother: "Does he miss his family?"

The child: "Yes."

Mother: "Can he still have thoughts?"

Child: "Yes."

Mother: "Does the cat's brain still work?"

Child: "No."

"How does that work?" the mother asks.

The body dies, but the mind lives on. Younger, more concrete children, before they construct this mind/body duality, may understand death to include corporeal immortality as well, and many religions preserve such early convictions. Sometimes the afterlife is a non-corporeal one, but in others actual bodily resurrection is anticipated: the dead rise and live again.

In any case, the logic of the dream is the logic of the unconscious and of childhood wishes; this is the logic by which people we know to be dead are dreamt of as living; in dreams, adult rationality coexists side-by-side with the magical thinking of childhood. I propose that the visual representations of dead persons in my dreams fulfills an unconscious childhood belief that the mind is immortal, and, perhaps, the body as well. The manifest content is that the dead person is not dead, has not died. The latent content is my own wish for immortality. If these admired figures can live forever, so can I. The dreamer's own wish for immortality is out of the dreamer's awareness, and therefore can be considered either unconscious or preconscious, accessible to consciousness on reflection.

But what does it mean to wish for immortality? By the end of latency children understand death as separation, and have begun to recognize it as inevitable, universal, and permanent. But death is unlike sexuality and aggression in the limits of our capacity to understand it fully. We do not have, and never will have, the opportunity to think back on what it felt like to be dead, and to bring our intellects to bear on the experience. Death remains forever unknown. I propose that this numinous quality, this enduring quiet menace is one reason that children's death-related fears and wishes are repressed along with sexual and aggressive ones, and relegated to the unconscious. Childhood ideas about death are no longer remembered, but return as hallucinatory wish fulfillments in dreams.

The cognitive aspects of this repression seem to be more complex than they are about the sexual and aggressive ambivalences. It takes a while for death's foreverness to become clear—if it ever entirely does. Even once older children begin to understand death as something feared by adults, they may still view it as something temporary or reversible. They do not understand that death is permanent for everyone. And—if I may use that metaphor—this belief dies very hard. Although it may be clear to adults in theory, we have no experiential basis on which to understand it emotionally, at least insofar as it applies to ourselves and not only as a matter of the loss of others. I recall bringing my bone box home as a medical student. My wife's grandfather, who was an orthodox Jew, worried about how these bones would be gathered when the Messiah returned, and all Jews returned to life. The persistence of such beliefs is why in Flannery O'Connor's *Wise Blood* the subversive preacher's profession of his religious credo is so unsettling: "The blind don't see, and the lame don't walk and what's dead stays that way!" (O'Connor, 1952). The dead stay dead even in a *religion???* Many of us talk to the people we have loved and lost as if they were alive even when we are awake; we really do know better, but... The permanence of death is not a given for anyone, no matter what age.

The point I want to make is that unlike sexual and aggressive wishes, feelings about death and immortality maintain a forbidden quality even in adult society. We all have crazy fantasies in which we talk to (or fight with) our dead parents. We see our long-dead cat's tail disappearing around a corner and think that it's time to refill his food bowl. We start trying to calculate how many years our savings are going to have to last, and we get freaked out. Most of us (with or without the help of analysis) get to the point where we understand sexuality and aggression pretty well. But we never quite figure out mortality, which we never get to experience with either cognition or consciousness at our disposal.

Fears of immortality. This incomplete grasp is something of a challenge even to adult reality testing, and makes it very hard to figure out which of our death-related thoughts can be fulfilled and which can't, which really are wishes and which are closer to fears. Certainly, the wish for longevity, let alone immortality, has its fearsome aspects; whatever our resistance to the idea of death, on some level we recognize that living forever is not a good alternative. It is better and more realistic to compromise, and aim for a long life. But *how* long? And under what circumstances? There are dangers there, too. Where death and longevity are concerned, it is very hard to draw the line between safe wishes and dangerous ones, and between what has to be repressed and what doesn't. Our relationship with mortality tests our capacity for reality testing in a way that other wishes don't. We do not necessarily grow into a comprehensive and sane adult view of death as we age, and I think that this too is a reason that some of our ideas about immortality and death remain more accessible in dreams than in other forms of awareness.

Schur (1972) writes, "The recognition that small children do not understand the meaning of death is the basis for Freud's eventual formulation that in our unconscious state, we know nothing about death in general and our own death in particular. Is this similar to the child not understanding why his sexual and aggressive Oedipal wishes can not be fulfilled?" That is a very hard question to answer, especially since we do not know to what extent a child's fear of acting on his sexual and aggressive Oedipal wishes does or doesn't equate to an understanding of "why" those wishes cannot be fulfilled. However unrealistic a child's understanding of exactly why he may not possess his mother may be, it is a very different order of not understanding from our inability to understand death, or so it seems to me. Wishes for immortality are unique in that they are the only wishes that can never be fulfilled. You can have sexual intercourse with your mother and survive. You can kill your father; people do. You can live a very long time. But...

The Fear that Haunts the Wish

Still, none of this explains why these concerns have to be kept permanently so far from consciousness that they present themselves to us only in dreams. If the wish for immortality is really as fundamental as sexual and aggressive wishes, if it really functions the same way in our psychology, what are the fears that keep it denied and repressed?

First of all, whether we understand them or not, our feelings about death are very, very complicated. I'll content myself with only a few examples of this:

* There are many literary depictions of the dangers of immortality; even the ultimate threat of western civilization—eternal damnation—loses its teeth with out the "eternal" part.

* Charlie Brenner points out that it is not necessarily wise to offer condolences to a newly bereaved person: "Maybe they're not sorry."

* Everybody achieves death, but how? I'm not worried about death, Woody Allen said. I just don't want to be there when it happens.

* Even Freud's personal grandiosity and passionate desire for immortality did not induce him to want to live forever. Once life became sufficiently exhausting and painful, he turned to suicide.

* Even if you do live forever, you won't know what to do at 2:30 on a Sunday afternoon.

The flip side of the wish for immortality is the fear of it—either one's own or that of others who wish us ill. If people live forever, we would like to think, we wouldn't have to feel guilty about any real or imagined deaths in which we are implicated. But this is only one side of the wish/fear coin.

113

Schur uses Freud's *"non-vixit"* dream to elaborate on these issues. In the dream, Ernst von Fleischl-Marxow is a revenant. Freud had introduced him to cocaine, which introduction eventually led to his death. A second revenant is Joseph Paneth, who took Freud's place as an assistant instructor in Brucke's laboratory. In the dream, both Joseph Paneth and Marxow, who are dead, are seen as alive. Fleiss, who is also in the dream, was still alive in real life. This dream (and the Irma dream) are generally seen as attempts on Freud's part to exculpate himself from the guilt of Marxow's death (and Irma's) by representing him (and her) as alive. It is also possible, however, to see Marxow's return as an accusation, against which Freud is still defending himself, to no avail. Immortality means that we can never hope for freedom from our accusers. They can always reproach us, and we can never definitively escape. Freud himself suggested that such revenants "existed as long as one liked and could've been gotten rid of if someone else wished it." But that appears to be a wish to which his own dream gives the lie; clearly Marxow and his reproaches have not been "gotten rid of" by Freud, and clearly the person who makes the dead person reappear is the dreamer.

In dreams, we don't have to invent ghosts, as we do in real life; there is no problem in representing immortality. Dreamers can undo death in fulfillment of childhood immortality wishes. But as always, this is a two-sided fulfillment. The continued existence of accusatory figures is a reproach to us; the conscious awareness of it is guilt. But the unconscious one is a wish for their death.

Standard interpretations of the *non-vixit* dream focus on Freud's Oedipal conflicts with his father; the two Josephs of the dream, Paneth and Breuer, were father figures too. But such interpretations look to me increasingly as though they enact with Freud his displacement of mortality issues onto concerns about sex and aggression, and his use of Oedipal preoccupations to push away a real analysis of the implications of Marxow's death. Am I out to lunch about this? Only further attention to immortality dreams will tell.

To pursue the analogy with sexual and aggressive wishes, we can note that immortality and longevity wishes and fears are represented in dreams in similar ways. A dream is almost always remembered upon waking as an image, a picture, a series of images. We see the dream in our mind's eye and remember the feelings that went with it. We start with the pictures. Only then do we think about what dreams may mean, using the tools that Freud has given us to unpack them: associations, the latent behind the manifest, and the concept of wish fulfillment. Otto Isakower used to warn candidates in the New York Psychoanalytic dream course about paying too much early attention to specific details. "Don't say to the patient, 'What does the dream as a whole, or each element in the dream, bring to mind?' But say, 'Let's have a look at it.'" His idea was to keep the patient in the visual dreaming mode. This is important. Immortality dreams can and must be understood as hallucinatory wish fulfillments as much as sexual and aggressive ones are.

Recently I had a dream the day residue of which was a discussion at the New York Psychoanalytic Institute about whom to invite to a retreat. I had complained about the marginalization of some senior members there, and also about my own exclusion for more than a decade from NYPSI activities. In the dream I was telling someone that they needed to invite or include Ernie Kafka, Sandy Abend (both of whom were living), Jack Arlow, and Charlie Brenner (both of whom were dead). The image in the dream is Brenner. He is alive, and he is speaking to me, but I don't recall his words. There is no image of Arlow.

Focusing on that image of Brenner telling me something, I associated to the way Jack and Charlie were marginalized at NYPSI in the forties and fifties by the European émigré analysts and their acolytes. Jack's response was to remove himself from the Institute. He didn't resign, but he became more involved with the Columbia Center and Downstate. Charlie stayed; and eventually he became an important mentor to the next generation. Now, in my frustration and anger at the Institute's marginalization of me, I found myself asking: Should I leave like Jack, or stay like Charlie? Presumably the image of Brenner, and not Jack, was telling me to stay.

On the other hand, the primary dream image is not always visual, and such variants can be noted in immortality dreams too. After Richard Gottlieb's death, a memorial was held for him at the New York Psychoanalytic Society. Richard had been in my class at the University of Chicago, and another classmate of ours, also a psychoanalyst, spoke of our shared background and shared heritage, and what the University of Chicago had stood for in our lives.

That was the day residue. That night, in a dream, I heard the voice of another friend, Fred Solomon, who had also been in our class at the U of C and who had also died within the last year. I felt as if I had a picture of him in my mind, but in the dream I did not actually see him. I did hear his voice, however, and he spoke for several minutes. I don't recall exactly what he said, only that his voice was as I remembered it; and I've had a sense since that what he was saying was something that I had heard him say before. This dream showed me that *hearing* the voice of a dead person also may represent the hallucinatory fulfillment of an immortality wish, but in the auditory rather than the visual mode.

A few words about immortality in trauma dreams. As I've mentioned, Freud's distinction between the wish-fulfillment dreams described in the *Interpretation of Dreams* and the traumatic dreams discussed in *Beyond the Pleasure Principle,* meets an interesting challenge in immortality dreams.

As I try to identify traumatic dreams of my own, two examples come to mind. The first are my recurrent dreams of concentration camps, in which I feel that there is no escape, and that I will be murdered. I've had these all my life, but at this point I am thinking about them differently. They relate to the traumatic realization of my childhood that six million Jews were murdered in Eastern Europe, including some of my own family. I had a very immediate connection with these events, having grown up in a Yiddish-speaking environment and reading Yiddish newspapers in which these cruel events were portrayed in vivid detail. I remember relating particular dreams to specific references to the Holocaust on the preceding day. But as I became more knowledgeable about psychoanalysis, I began to look for latent sexual and aggressive wishes, oedipal or otherwise, for which I was being punished, and to note that the very fact of being punished for the wishes meant that they had been gratified: the disguised latent wish under the manifest content. I also recall feeling in these dreams that they were only dreams after all, that the dream was not really happening, and that I would wake up feeling relieved.

But in this new context I note that although these dreams were literally about life and death, I was scrutinizing them, as per Freud's example, not for the meaning of that, but for sexual and aggressive content. That awareness has led to a different interpretation of the latent content and the wish it disguises: my relatives died, and I'm still alive. The joy of my good fortune, in other words, and its seamy side—survivor guilt.

A second familiar category of traumatic dreams are those in which I dream about someone close to me who has died. These are different from the dreams I cited earlier because painful affect is associated with the presence of the dead person. Richard Gottlieb, whose memorial service I mentioned above, died last year at a relatively young age, after a rapid and terrible encounter with cancer and its treatment. He was very dear to me, and for four or five successive nights I had dreams in which he appeared. I would see him and try to convey to him that he should not be there, because he is dead; I would feel anxious and upset, but he doesn't listen. Waking, I can experience his death as the trauma it was and the dream as an effort to undo and master it by visually representing

117

him as alive. I know that I cannot bring him to life permanently, but for a short while, in the dream time, I can.

This dream reminds me of others, in which my father is alive, and I maintain him to be so in my dream so that he and I may both experience my oedipal triumph, which is that he is dead and I am not. The guilt of the wish, and the fear of the punishment it evokes, are neatly counterbalanced by the gift of immortality that I offer him.

I contend that the wish for immortality, or perhaps more accurately in this case the denial of death, is the underlying wish that is fulfilled in this dream, and that this is consistent with both the first and second of Freud's dream theories. Immortality dreams are fascinating in the intimacy with which they link these two categories of dreams that Freud separated so definitively. The trauma and the fulfillment of the wish are one and the same, and so are the mastery of the trauma and the reason for the suppression of the wish.

Longevity dreams seem to me to be a subset of immortality dreams in that they do not explicitly deny death, but they take an active stance against it. Furthermore, wishes for longevity, unlike immortality wishes, are frequently conscious, and sometimes possible of fulfillment. Shortly after the memorial service dream recounted above I had one involving Jack Arlow and Leo Stone, both of whom were dead at the time but alive in the dream. They were looking for new offices. I saw a building that they were considering—still only a framework that had not yet been completed. There was a visual image of Jack in the dream, but none of Leo. One aspect of the day residue was riding in the elevator at the NYPSI where the memorial for Richard Gottlieb was being held, and seeing the list of analysts in newly renovated offices there. I had the thought that if I were starting a practice, having an office at the institute would be nice—turning the clock back and being a young man again.

The Leo Stone day residue had to do with my impending

publication of a book whose title was *The Widening Scope of Psychoanalysis and Psychotherapy* (the title, or course, inspired by Stone); the author was ill, and I was hoping he would manage to complete this work in his lifetime. And in mine? What will I manage to complete before my time is up?

I can offer two more dreams that seem to address the wish for longevity directly. One is similar to the dream of the unfinished offices. I am driving a Renault Dauphine, the car that we owned in 1958. Our grandson, now thirty, was in the passenger seat. The day residue had to do with new developments in his life, specifically the possibility that he may get married and have children. The very reminder of children and grandchildren is, in its way, a fulfillment of the immortality wish. But the wish to turn the clock back—to be young again ourselves—is evident too; if we can return to 1958 at will, we can essentially live forever.

In the second dream I am going to a cemetery to unveil a tombstone for my father, who had just died. (In fact he died in 1975.) The day residue was that I had just noted in a biography of Isakower that he was born in 1899, the year after my father. Now it was 2018; in the dream, my father lived to be 120.

Discussion

Freud thought that beliefs in previous lives, transmigration of souls, and reincarnation are all products of the denial of death. Implicit in this denial is the wish for immortality, which he considered a universal experience "in the unconscious every one of us is convinced of his own immortality" (Freud, 1915. p. 288). In my view, however, we begin not with a wish for, but with a *belief in* immortality. This is a child's view until age four. It is given up with some reluctance, and endures for a while as a cognitive/corporeal split, not so different from a phenomenon that Freud recognized: "In reaction to death of someone close, the primitive man invented other forms of existence, such as spirits and ghosts." The idea of life after death is a reflection of our persistent memory of the dead, and Freud believed that the creation of religion is related to illusory wishes projected by the living in the face of death, by an unconscious in which there is "no sense of the process of time."

Yet he did not include these powerful wishes and illusions as foundational in *The Interpretation of Dreams*. He does include some dreams in which immortality wishes are evident, yet he seems to give them short shrift. Why did he exclude them, and the terrifying implications of their denial, in his catalog of the motivating wishes of the human animal? Let me offer a few speculations.

One possible explanation is that he thought that it was his views of childhood sexuality and the Oedipus complex that were his major discovery. This fits in with the epigraph he chose for the book—about shaking the underworld. Yet that view just reemphasizes his own immense preoccupation with immortality, and his inability to face directly his own inevitable death.

Another possibility is that the awareness of death is an ego-based, cognitive, and rational experience. Unlike the visceral passions of desire and rage, it is available to us (insofar as it *is* available to us) only through ego-modulated experiences of cognition and memory. As we mature and become accustomed to passion, we increasingly master it. But death can never be mastered, and the more fully we grasp its reality, the more terrifying it is to face. Freud's interest in Fliess's (1904) numerological protocol for predicting the age of his death (61 or 62) reflects, in my view, a reaction formation to this awareness, an attempt to deny his helplessness in the face of his ultimate undoing, by means of a prediction that he hoped would not be fulfilled. The fear of death is why the wish for immortality, which it underlies, had to be omitted from his catalog of wishes.

A third possibility is that, as we have noted, wishes for longevity tend to be conscious, while the fears—of death and of life without it—tend not to be. Freud asserted not only that we cannot imagine our own deaths, but that our own deaths are not represented in the unconscious (Freud, 1900). Therefore, he did not consider either whether personal wishes for immortality—or, in some circumstances, for death—can in fact be represented in dreams as the sexual and aggressive wishes are, or if death might be dreamed of as a trauma to be mastered through repetition. I propose, though, that while we cannot fully imagine death, we can fear it and we can long for it, and that we *do* fear it and sometimes long for it, and that those fears and longings are stimulated by our conscious and unconscious experiences of illness, accident, and what we observe as the death-experiences of others. On balance the wish for longevity lies closer to consciousness, and the wishes for immortality and for death lie deeper. But I believe that both of these wishes can be represented in both kinds of dreams.

I conclude with a question. How do these ideas relate to our clinical work? As I was completing the first draft of this paper, I was asked to offer some clinical examples of dreams that were not my own. I couldn't recall a patient's dream in which a wish for immortality, or a preoccupation with longevity, was evident. However, I do not conclude from this that such dreams were never reported; only that I did not recognize them at the time, as I failed for many years to recognize that aspect of my concentration camp dreams. This may have been true of Freud too; he taught us, and we learned from him, to focus in the clinical setting on the ambivalence conflicts of children, on Brenner's "four calamities," (Brenner, 1982) and on other such concerns. Like most of us, my clinical attention has been to pathological object relations, projective identification, denial, repression, and displacement. And immortality in dreams seems (on the surface, at least) to be less "hot" a subject than sex and aggression, and much less dramatic.

But now I wonder about this. Perhaps these dreams are "invisible" in part because we have far less power to negotiate our death-related passions than our sexual and aggressive ones. And while we understand our own aggression and sexuality better as we mature, in some ways death becomes harder to grapple with the closer we get to it. The sexual and competitive passions slacken a bit as we age, but death becomes ever more preoccupying and distracting.

The threat of death is a reality that can never be mastered or contained or mentalized or symbolized. As Time's wingèd chariot approaches, we realize ever more clearly that our earlier "understanding" of death was incomplete; we left out the recognition that it is aiming *at us*. Death is a fundamental preoccupation, and so unnerving that perhaps even oedipal catastrophe appears safer than looking it in the face. It comes when it comes. It comes how it comes. You can survive abandonment and castration. But you can't survive death.

The *wish* for immortality is ubiquitous, or nearly so. Goodreads cites 434 quotes on the subject from a wide range of authors. Fears come with it, although we don't always think about them much: what if Irma *did* return? What if an angry Marxow *did* come back? What if there really was no escape from great age, from illness, from dementia, from pain? Such wishes and fears cannot survive the rational processes of our conscious minds, but they do survive in the irrational unconscious, where the rules of logic and reality do not prevail. I have tried to show that they display the same status and relationship to reality as the sexual and aggressive wishes of childhood: they are fearful and ambivalent wishes experienced and dangerous enough to require repression. Immortality wishes and fears may provide even clearer demonstrations of Freud's theories than the familiar sexual and aggressive ones do, because unlike the latter they can never be tested out, gratified, or mastered.

But while these wishes and fears may be universal, the conscious *belief* in immortality—that is, the idea that a person can live forever—is not universal at all. Yes, there are religious doctrines of eternal life, and of corporeal reincarnation, and of a soul or spirit that survives the death of the body. But immortality as a real possibility is a belief that children deconstruct and abandon as their cognition and their egos mature. The unconscious remnant that is left of it, I submit, is a wish and a fear about what existence would be like if the terrifying fact of death were not so.

The awareness of life and death are organizing forces of our psychic lives as powerful any others (and let me point out that our fears of our sexual and aggressive desires would be far less daunting if Death were not an active construct in our awareness). They are as conflicted and as subject to ambivalence as any of our other major psychic experiences, as likely therefore to be subject to repression, and so as likely to appear ultimately in dreams as any of these others. However, we know that Freud, by his own admission, often stopped short in his dream analyses. He did not want to reveal too much about himself to his readers, and given some of his comments in other areas, we can wonder too whether perhaps to some extent he preferred to be blind himself to the area that mattered to him most.

In his work on dreams, he cast a great light upon a universal and mysterious human experience, and it is in a spirit of appreciation that I avail myself of the opportunity here to shine that light into a corner that he missed. I suggest that the wish for immortality shares the childhood origin, and the fate, of early sexual and aggressive oedipal wishes, and I propose that they be added now to his inventory of primary dream wishes. I hope profoundly that as we further explore this topic, both theoretically and clinically, we will find the evidence for a greatly enhanced understanding of immortality wishes and their place in, and contribution to, our dreams.

References

Brenner, C. (1982). The Concept of the Superego: A Reformulation. *Psychoanalytic Quarterly* 51:501–525.

Freud, S. (1900). The Interpretation of Dreams *Standard Edition* 4:ix–627.

—— (1904). *The Complete Letters of Sigmund Freud to Wilhelm Fliess, 1887–1904,* ed. Jeffrey Masson. Cambridge: Belknap Press, 1986.

——(1920). Beyond the Pleasure Principle. *Standard Edition* 18:1–64.

—— (1915). Thoughts For The Times On War And Death. *Standard Edition* 14:273–300.

Kardiner, A. Karush, A., & Ovesey, L., (1959). A Methodological Study of Freudian Theory: Ii. The Libido Theory. *The Journal of Nervous and Mental Disease* 129 (2):133–143.

O'Connor, F. (1952). *Wise Blood: A Novel.* New York: Harcourt, Brace & Company.

Olson, K.R. (2013). Children's Understanding of Death and the Afterlife: Evidence for "natural-born dualism"? *Psychology Today,* December 12, 2013.

Richards, A.D. (1996) Freud's Theory of Motivation and Others, In: *Psychoanalytic at the Political Border: Essays in Honor of Rafael Moses.* Edited by Leo Rangell and Rena Moses Hrushaovski, Madison, CT: International Universities Press.

Schur, M. (1972) *Freud: Living and Dying.* Madison, CT: International Universities Press.

The Interpretations of Dreams in Clinical Work (Workshop Series of the American Psychoanalytic Association, Monograph 3): Introduction (1987). (78): pp. xiii–xvi.

Arnold Rothstein

Psychoanalytic mythology teaches us that psychoanalysis was born in the crucible of Freud's self-analysis. The primary data and experience of that creative self-analytic enterprise were Freud's dreams, culminating in his discovery of infantile sexuality in his (1900) analysis of the Irma dream.[1] The topographic model of the mind that resulted emphasized the paradigm of discovering the repressed latent wish behind the manifest facade.

---

[1] The dream of "Irma's injection" was dreamt by Freud on July 23 to 24, 1895. It is a characteristic of the mythologizing of discovery to conceive of a particular discovery as having occurred at one particular moment. Creation and discovery are more accurately described as processes occurring over time and characterized by nodal points of insight. In fact, Freud had earlier, in a letter to Fliess of March 4, 1895, described a wishful "dream of convenience" dreamt by Breuer's nephew Rudi Kaufman (Freud, 1887–1902).

The purpose of the workshop from which this book originated was the discussion of the clinical significance of the interpretation of dreams. The focus is the collaborative therapeutic situation rather than the solitary creative self-analytic endeavor. In the twenty-seven years following Freud's analysis of the Irma dream, his clinical experience influenced him to emend his theory of dream formation and his corresponding model of the mind. In 1919 (Freud, 1900, pp. 557–558), Freud described the gratification of a wish for punishment as a motive for creating a dream, presaging his (1923a) formal introduction of the structural hypothesis and adding the superego to the id as an instigator of dreaming. In 1920, in describing an "original function" of the dream work, Freud added a third factor, the ego, to the list of motives contributing to the mind's penchant for creating dreams. In regard to the ego's "original function" Freud was moving "Beyond the Pleasure Principle" and the wish fulfilling function of dreaming and emphasizing the ego as a structure of adaptation working to assimilate trauma. Analytic work also influenced Freud (1911, 1923b) to deemphasize the uniqueness of dreams. He came to conceive of dreams as data to be dealt with as part of that process and warned against the urge to think of the analysis of dreams as an art to be pursued for its own intrinsic pleasure. Debate about this point persists to this day. In addition, in the same year that Freud (1923a) formally introduced the structural hypothesis, he (1923b) legitimized "dreams from above." Thus, Freud's ultimate view was, as Brenner's (1982) work has emphasized; namely, that dreams, like all other products of the mind, are to be thought of as compromise formations. Dreams are fantasies created by contributions from the three agencies of the mind.

In the sixty years since Freud's last contribution to this subject, numerous authors have questioned his emphasis on the wish fulfilling function of dreaming. Some (Spanjäard, 1969) have emphasized clinicians' tendencies to make more of the manifest content of dreams than traditional theory would suggest advisable, while others have stressed one or another aspect of the assimilative or adaptive aspects of the dream work. Some colleagues (Greenberg and Pearlman, 1978) have studied dreams in sleep laboratories and emphasized the manifest content and adaptive aspects of dreaming, while others (Polombo, 1976) have made similar points from other nonclinical perspectives such as those that stress the mind's memory and information processing functions.

Waelder (1930) and Erikson (1954), from an ego psychological perspective, stressed the complexity of the dream. Waelder explored the dream from the perspective of "the principle of multiple function" (p. 59). Erikson described the complexity of the surface of the reported dream. Erikson suggested the term *manifest configuration* to more accurately connote the complex nature of the data available in the manifest dream. He provided a rich schema for organizing the links between the more manifest and more latent elements in dreams.

The editor raised the following questions for the contributors to this work with the intention of facilitating the development of their presentations: In work with dreams, how does the analyst think about the dream as presented by the patient? In that regard, how does the analyst's theoretical commitments and/or data available from other than clinical experience influence his understanding of the patient's dreams? How does the analyst conceptualize the relationships between the manifest and latent content of the dream? Does the analyst think of dreams as a unique type of clinical data? In that regard, does the analysis of dreams provide a unique opportunity for insight and integration? Is the analysis of dreams particularly helpful in working with certain kinds of issues, such as the reconstruction of trauma or the recovery of masturbatory fantasies, or particular types of patients such as those prone to enactment and acting out or those thought of as "borderline" or "narcissistic"? Does the patient's ability to analyze his or her own dreams offer unique evidence of a successful treatment and is it a positive prognostic indicator of successful postanalytic self-analysis? Finally, do the contributors think of dreams differently when doing psychoanalysis as compared to psychoanalytic psychotherapy?

The Interpretations of Dreams in Clinical Work (Workshop Series of the American Psychoanalytic Association, Monograph 3): Chapter 14 Conclusion (1987). (78):197–203.

Arnold Rothstein

In concluding this third volume of the Workshop Series of the American Psychoanalytic Association I am aware of a continuity with what I noted in concluding the first two volumes of the series. In addition, I am reminded that one of the goals of this concluding chapter is to make a statement of the state of the question(s) that served as the facilitating frame of reference for the workshop that resulted in this monograph.

In 1985, I began the concluding chapter to *Models of the Mind: Their Relationships to Clinical Work* by noting that:

In writing these concluding remarks I am acutely aware that my commitments to the structural hypothesis and to a meta-theoretical perspective on its evolutionary development significantly influence my experience of the alternative theories upon which I am about to comment. ... Nevertheless, I have been able to "try a theory on," to immerse myself in it in an attempt to experience its usefulness in analytic work. These experiences have convinced me that there is considerable value in thinking about what might be helpful in the ideas of colleagues with whom I have considerable disagreement.

In reading the contributions to this book it is clear that each author has a more or less defined model of the mind that organizes his concept of the dream work and his theory of *technique;* that is, each author has a psychological theory and a derivative theory of what the mind of the patient is doing while he is sleeping and dreaming and what the therapist should or should not do with reported dreams in their clinical work.

At this point I will briefly outline the model of the mind that organizes my clinical work with *dreams.* This outline can then serve as a frame of reference for the comments that comprise the remainder of this chapter. My model draws heavily on Freud (1900, 1914a, 1923a, 1926, and 1937), Waelder (1930), Arlow and Brenner (1964), and Brenner (1982). (For a more detailed statement of my understanding of the structural hypothesis and its relationship to the dream work, see Rothstein [1983].) In my view the structural hypothesis suggests the metapsychological premise that the mind is comprised of structures (id, ego, superego) that organize the experience of mental life. The phrase "mental life" refers to an individual's fantasies (conscious/unconscious) that have ideational and affective components. From this perspective all fantasies and their derivative enactments are conceived of as compromise formations created by contributions of these structures. The dream and all other data of the clinical situation are viewed, from this perspective, as compromised formations.

In reading the contributions to this book and the summary of the spontaneous discussions, it is clear that many colleagues are interested in the concept of trauma and in the function of the dream work in assimilating trauma. My view of psychological trauma is quite similar to that described by Dowling in chapter 4 of this monograph and in greater detail in his

(1986) contribution to *The Reconstruction of Trauma: Its Significance in Clinical Work.* From that perspective psychological trauma is defined by the meanings attributed to an experience by an individual.

I conceive of a so-called traumatic dream as I would think of any manifest dream: as a compromise formation. If a manifest dream reported immediately after a trauma portrays solely the traumatic incident and is accompanied by intense anxiety approximating a nightmare, I understand the most obvious aspect of dream work to be the mechanism of repetition that Freud (1920) described under the rubric of the "original function" of the dream work. The ego in the dream work is attempting to assimilate the disturbing affect and simultaneously to create the illusion of undoing the experience. The therapist's response is similarly aimed at facilitating the ego's assimilation of the disturbing experience. At first this may consist solely of listening to the dream in an appropriately therapeutic manner. However, my perspective on the dream work suggests that it is characterized by a number of mechanisms subsumed under the rubric of its multiple functions. The proposal that the ego in the dream work is attempting to create the illusion of undoing the experience conceives of a wish fulfilling motive as an intrinsic aspect of the ego's efforts at assimilation. I (1983) have suggested that there is a gratifying restoration of a fantasy of narcissistic perfection for the "self representation as agent" associated with the illusion of undoing and/or being in control of an experience. I have described this narcissistic identificatory aspect of the dream work under the rubric of a "narcissistic function" (Rothstein, 1983, pp. 137–139) of the dream work and conceived of this function as a "bridge" between the original and wish fulfilling functions of the dream work. This perspective on the dream work emphasizes that the mind's structures are continually organizing and interpreting experience. This psychological elaboration of the experience considered traumatic accounts for the fact that many so-called traumatic manifest dreams portray the trauma in some subtly changed manner. It is the associations to these elaborations in the manifest dream that facilitate insight into the more latent and unique personal meanings of an experience to an individual. Thus, although a therapist may choose to focus on the assimilation of the disturbing affective component of a reported dream, he is aware that the subtle elaborations of the manifest content lead to more latent meanings organized by a variety of dream work mechanisms including those of condensation, displacement, and symbolization that Freud (1900) first described under the wish fulfillment function of the dream work. Finally, in my experience, it is often the analysis of the unconscious guilt associated with the individual's interpretation of a traumatic experience that facilitates a diminution in the frequency and intensity of repetitive "traumatic" dreams.

An important focus of the workshop that resulted in this book was an exploration of the value of the manifest content. Virtually all the contributors placed some value on the manifest content, and many seemed to employ it in their daily work in a manner that Spanjäard (1969) suggested: "to evaluate the most superficial layer of the conflict" (p. 224). However, from my perspective there was a tendency in some of the chapters to make more of the manifest content than I believe is warranted. In that regard I suggest it is misleading to give a dream a label, such as a "self-state" or "traumatic" dream or a dream of "mourning," "separation," "loss," "termination," or "of the analytic undisguised." Such labels tend to imply a unifactorial dynamic in the *construction* of the dream that organizes the therapist's attention and may inhibit further exploration of the meanings of the dream. For example, so-called repetitive dreams of mourning which deal, in part, with the assimilation of loss also deal with a panoply of related meanings, such as unconscious aggressive wishes toward the deceased and associated guilt. The repetitive nature of these dreams may be influenced as much by a need to expiate guilt as it is to mourn.

Bradlow has pursued a truly original methodology to explore the value of the manifest dream for prediction in psycho-analysis and *psychoanalytic psychotherapy*. Although most colleagues applauded Bradlow's efforts, many would be cautious about making generalizations from manifest dreams. A number of colleagues gave examples of successful work with patients who had manifest dreams of the kind that Bradlow suggested were associated with a guarded prognosis. While I also applaud Bradlow's efforts, a number of cautionary notes are indicated. There is a question of the influence of an analyst's interest in prediction, analyzability evaluations, and questions of diagnosis on the evolving opening phase of treatment. My own view of these efforts is that they may subtly affect an analyst's attitude and may hinder trials of analysis with selected sensitive patients.

In addition, Bradlow presents the manifest content of *dreams* as if it were equivalent to the latent content. He describes a "murder dream" as if it were a direct expression of "severe impounded rage" and implicitly makes strong inferences concerning impaired and possibly unanalyzable character structure. In that regard, in response to a manifest dream of "sexual activity between family members" Bradlow notes, "A failure of the synthetic function of the ego might be involved."

While it is certainly true, as Rangell noted, that, "Trivialities during the day are unable to pursue us in our sleep", it seems clear that disturbing events of the dream day can. Thus, "dreams from above" reflect, in part, the ego in the dream work attempting to assimilate disturbing experiences of the day. However, these disturbing events are often experienced as contemporary narcissistic injuries and resonate with the narcissistic injuries of childhood. In the discussion of "self-state dreams" Ornstein discussed his patients' dreams as if they were solely "dreams from above"; that is exclusively created in response to disturbing events of the dream day.

Ornstein presented Kohut's concept of the "self-state" dream as a dream with a different structure and function: "the bind[ing of] the non-verbal tensions of traumatic states" (Kohut, 1971, p. 108). What was, in 1971, a type of dream has become for Ornstein in 1986 a revolutionary alternative to traditional dream theory. Ornstein stated: "It is this elevation of the … regulatory, and restorative function of dreams to a supraordinate position in dream psychology … that has radically transformed dream theory and the understanding of dreams in the clinical situation" (p. 103).

I would suggest that Ornstein's model of the mind and its resulting "dream psychology" creates a technique, a methodology of clinical work, that is radically different from the methodology of colleagues working from a conflict model. Rather than discovering a new dream, Ornstein's supraordinate interest in restitution promotes a radical shift of attention in the clinical situation. His interest in the expression of subtle or not so subtle shifts of integration and his responses aimed at facilitating "restitution," influence him to be less interested in the latent meanings of dreams. Therefore it is not so much as Kohut suggests of "self-state" dreams that there are objectively no further deepening associations to a dream, but that for an analyst working with a dream from the perspective of psychology of the self, there are no further deepening associations to certain dreams, while to an analyst working from a traditional perspective that stresses the interminability of conflict there are always further deepening associations which he may or may not choose to pursue.

In that regard concepts like "defect" and "fragmentation," and the clinical data often attributed to them such as a patient's tension laden states or sense of void and/or complaints of feeling empty, are conceived, like "self-state" dreams, as end states. I would emphasize that these concepts and the related clinical states of mind can be thought of as manifest content, as fantasies that can be associated to in order to explore their more latent and overdetermined meanings.

Finally, a great deal of discussion focused on the question, "Is the dream a special kind of data?" It was clear that many colleagues felt a particular attraction for dreams. In addition to the many factors cited to explain this phenomenon, it may be that dreams are an important focus of many analysts' ongoing self-analyses. It is equally clear that colleagues were aware that whatever their personal or scientific interest in dreams, if that interest is excessive, it certainly can influence their clinical work and the dreams reported in it. In that regard, the principle of neutrality provides a clinical ideal that can facilitate a more optimal attention to all the data of the analytic experience.

In concluding Monograph 1 of this series, it was clear "that significant disagreement exists and questions remain relating to our understanding of the relationships of preoedipal to oedipal and postoedipal experience" (Rothstein, 1985, p. 135). In concluding Monograph 2 I noted:

> This book clearly demonstrates that although colleagues use the same terms to describe what they do, these terms have a variety of meanings. It is also likely that different colleagues function differently in their clinical work. It seems probable that within the term analysis there are a number of analyses practiced by a variety of analysts for a spectrum of patients (1986, p. 229).

These differences are relevant to considerations of the differences of emphasis encountered in the various contributions to this volume. It is clear from these contributions that analysts think differently about dreams and work differently with them in their clinical practice. Significant differences exist concerning the value of the manifest content of the dream and concerning the interpretation of a dream as a "concrete puzzle solution" within a given paradigmatic perspective. One colleague might focus on facilitating "restitution" while another might choose to interpret resistance and pursue latent meanings. In the pursuit of meaning one colleague might listen to the associations to a dream from a perspective that organizes data in a manner that favors reconstruction of hypothesized preo-edipal trauma with resulting arrests of development while another might listen from an organizing perspective that favors oedipal interpretations. The latter would emphasize the centrality of conflict and compromise formation and would interpret one or another aspect of the compromise: drive, defense, and/or the influence of conscience. At this time in the history of psychoanalysis we are confronted with the fact that no sound research methodology exists for re-solving the differences that characterize our field and which are demonstrated in this volume. The development of addi-tional research perspectives beyond the analytic method it-self could help explore a number of questions raised by the discussions of the workshops. It would be interesting to study the influence of the analyst's personality on his choice and interpretation of his theory or theories. In addition, it would be interesting to compare processes of a number of analysts working with dreams from a variety of clinical perspectives.

Finally, future scientific meetings will contribute to the clari-fication of some of the questions raised in this book. The 1986 Workshop for Mental Health Professionals on "The Mode of Therapeutic Action of Psychoanalytic Psychotherapy, or How Does Treatment Help?" is of particular value in this regard.

The preceding two articles were submitted without references. For the reference lists, see the original volume, *Rothstein, A. ed (1987). The Interpretations of Dreams in Clinical Work* (Workshop Series of the American Psychoanalytic Association, Monograph 3).

Freud's Interpretations in the Dora Case: A Compendium

Arnold D. Richards

The Dora Case

Freud provided a particularly detailed analysis of two dreams in his Dora case. In the Dora case Freud moves primarily from theory to interpretation in his analysis of Dora's symptoms. In section 2, with the first dream, the sequence is reversed. He starts by presenting the manifest content of the dream. He then discusses its recurrent quality and delineates the day residue both recent and remote. He next establishes the connection between the dream's manifest content and the important events that occurred at L., the place on the lake where the scene with Herr K. had taken place. The first three "playings of the dream" had to do with Dora's response to Herr K.'s overtures, her efforts to fend off his advances, to lock the room while she was asleep until she had the opportunity to leave the house and sleep without fear of Herr K.'s intrusions. Through the analysis of the dream Freud was able to establish motivation and reconstruct some past events, and it is only after this bit of analytic detective work that Freud turns to theory as laid out in his dream book.

Freud accepts the possibility that the analysis of Dora's dream, which had revealed "the continuation into sleep of an intention formed during the day," might also reveal the operation of the presence of a wish represented as fulfilled. The road into the interior is the jewel case. Her mother is fond of jewelry and her father gives her mother a lot of it. Her mother didn't want a particular gift but she, Dora, would have accepted it with pleasure. From the technical 'point of view this is a direct interpretation. Freud makes an interpretive leap, without Dora's associations. The inference is based partly on Freud's conviction about the validity of his theory of the Oedipus complex: every little girl would like to get from father the same thing he gives mother. To strengthen his case, he refers to his theory of symbolism. The jewel case is the symbol for the female genital. The oedipal protagonists, Dora's father and mother, are stand-ins for the current life protagonists, Herr K. and his wife. Herr K. is represented in the dream as wanting in on Dora' s jewel case.

Freud evokes the rule of opposites. Negative becomes positive, the oedipal fear becomes the oedipal wish, and the oedipal wish defends upward against her wish for her current day admirer. Freud finds in the dream Dora's struggle with her sexual drives. Freud pays the price for his directness and his failure to elicit more of the patient's associations. "Dora would not follow me in this part of the interpretation." Freud, rebuffed. turns to his theory, the theory of dream formation lined out in *The Interpretation of Dreams*. "The dream sets up a connection between these two factors, the event during childhood and the event of the present day. And it endeavors to reshape the present on the model of the remote past . ... The wish that creates the dream always springs from the period of childhood and it is continually trying to summon childhood back into reality and to correct the present day by the measure of childhood."

Freud reports in a footnote that at the end of this last session, the reappearance of the dream forced him to conclude that Dora intended to leave treatment. Freud does not tell us why he decides the next time he sees Dora not to bring up his concern about her departure, but instead decides to pursue a line of exploration that he tells us is "indispensable both for the amnesia of the case and for the theory of dreams." But, we might add, not felicitous for the continuation of the treatment. Freud seems not to be listening to his patient. He moves the analysis off the verbal mode and instead decides to conduct a "little experiment." He forces her attention away from her own thoughts and from the dream and onto an object in the room, a match stand on the table that, even when asked, Dora does not notice particularly. Freud knows that he must somehow get to a childhood event to demonstrate that his theory about the centrality of repressed childhood sexual wishes in the formation of the dream is valid and can be demonstrated in the case of Dora's dream, like in any other.

In order to reach this goal, Freud has to provide the rails for his theoretical train and finds it in symbolic and linguistic connections of fire and water, leading to love and bedwetting, and Freud's journey stops when he reaches the sought for reconstruction. Dora was "addicted to bedwetting" up to a later age than is usual for children. This was also true for her brother and her father woke her up in the middle of the night to take her to the bathroom to prevent her from wetting her bed. And "Dora," says Freud, "what have your recollections to say to this?" Dora obliges Freud by confirming both her brother's bedwetting and her own. Freud ends this session satisfied with his analytic efforts. "The interpretation of the dream now seems to be complete. The latent content is "the temptation is so strong, dear father, protect me again as you used to in my childhood and prevent my bed from being wetted."

It is striking that Freud does not tell us whether or not he conveyed this interpretation directly to Dora or how she responded. This may be why in the very next session Dora tells Freud about something that she had forgotten to relate about the dream, in an effort, perhaps, to return Freud to the text of her dream; to move him from his theory to her experience. Dora had forgotten to relate that each time after waking up she had smelled smoke. Freud correctly refers to the transference; he is a smoker. But, says Dora, she smelled smoke before she met Freud. Freud makes a theoretical/technical point. The smell of smoke comes as an addendum to the drama. This suggests that it "had to overcome a particularly strong effort on the part of repression." The temptation had to do with the dream wish, the wish to yield to Herr K., or more properly, to Dora's forbidden trinity—father, Herr K., and Freud.

Freud points out in a masterful intuitive leap the idea that the transference, the wish to have him kiss her, must have served as the day residue, the recent instigator of the dream. Freud said, "This would have been the exciting cause which led her to repeat the warning dream and form her intention of stopping the treatment. Clearly, transference is resistance! Freud continues, "Everything fits together very satisfactorily upon this view, but owing to the characteristics of 'transference,' its validity is not susceptible of definite proof." Freud makes us aware of a fundamental issue in regard to his new concept. The concept of transference is theoretical, abstract, experience-distant, and not susceptible to definitive proof. Transference was discovered by Freud and not simply observed. Transference is not a theory-free observation, Freud recognizes that he has to make up his mind as to whether he should focus on what his case illuminates about his theory of dreams or what his theory of dreams illuminates about the case. He decides on the latter rather than the former. He puts practice before theory. But he begins by focusing on early history and development and on certain theoretical considerations rather than the dream's text.

The clinical phenomenon of the childhood disorder is the recurrence of bedwetting after Dora's sixth year. Bedwetting is connected with masturbation, and childhood masturbation is the pathogenetic smoking gun of hysteria. Freud views the case through the prism of his early theories, the pathogenic roles of hereditary disposition, childhood sexual trauma, and sexual "malpractice." The constitutional factor is syphilis. Dora is aware of her father's illness. Dora relates her difficulty to her father's syphilis but confuses syphilis and gonorrhea; syphilis is congenital, gonorrhea is contagious. Dora identifies with her mother; her mother's medical condition (venereal disease), and her mother's personality, "peculiarities of manner," and "intolerable behavior."

Freud then shifts to psychology. He proposes that Dora's accusations about her father conceal a self-accusation. The mechanism is "I accuse you of being bad because I feel bad myself." This is the melancholic defense. Guilt is central and guilt suggests masturbation. Freud expected that Dora would confess or otherwise confirm his speculation about her childhood masturbation, but "Dora denied flatly that she could remember any such thing." But Freud doesn't give in. Seek and ye shall find. Freud finds his proof, Dora's "symptomatic act," her reticule play. Dora wears the reticule because it is the fashion, she says. But Freud insists the reticule is the female genital and reticule playing is masturbation. Freud's evidence is his clinical experience. He has a "series of symptomatic acts." He gives us one example from an analytic session.

Freud uses symbolism to interpret symptomatic acts and does not follow his own dictum that symbolic interpretations in dreams are the interpretations of last resort. He does not give Dora an opportunity to associate to her behavior, expecting that meaning will emerge. Freud interprets Dora's concealment of her letter as her wish to "play secrets." Freud presses to proving his case against Dora without sufficient attention to the unwillingness of his patient to be enlightened. Dora's skepticism contrasts sharply with Freud's certainty. His case to him is "complete and without a flaw." Freud is out of touch with his patient. Indicative is the reference to Wilhelm Fliess and his gastric spot. Freud shifts to more solid clinical ground: the chronology of Dora's symptom picture. Dora reports that when her bedwetting stopped, her nervous asthma appeared. Freud invoked a general principle: hysterical symptoms and childhood masturbation are incompatible.

They are mutually exclusive. Symptom involves drive gratification, some variant of masturbation. This idea is a part of
the current compromise formation theory of neurosis. The
relation between Freud's theory of actual neurosis and the in-
verse relation between sexual practice and symptomatology
and our modern-day view of compromise formation should
be noted. Inadequate sexual gratification in adulthood as in
coitus interruptus is equivalent to masturbatory abstinence
in childhood. Both lead to hysterical symptoms. "The libido
flows back again into its old channel."

A brilliant *tour-de-force* analysis of a childhood symptom of Dora's dyspnia follows. Freud provides us
with the detailed sequence of its development. His
reconstruction was derived partly from material
obtained directly from the analysis, but "the rest required
supplementing." Included here are references and connections based on the specific sequence of events in Dora's case
as well as more general propositions about children's responses to primal scene exposure, valid for everyone. The
mix of the universal and the particular and the interplay
between the two is very nicely presented in this portion of
Freud's exposition.

Freud, stressing the centrality of infantile masturbation as
an etiological root of hysteria, indicates that he has replaced
a seduction/actual neurosis view of neurosogenesis with one
in which unconscious fantasy is central. Freud may be aware
of the shakiness of his explanatory and expository ground.
He refers to "a whole series of questions which arise concerning the etiology of hysteria." Freud is at his theoretical worst
and out of touch with his patient. But he gets back on track
in the footnote on p. 82 in which he discusses the relationship between Dora and her brother and how that impacted
on her own school performance. The shift from being wild to
becoming quiet and well behaved and how that is related to
the onset of asthma raises interesting issues.

Freud is on firmer ground when he uses lexical and

psychological principles to analyze Dora's symptom, her ca-tarrh/cough. He provides an intricate account of the etiologic layering in the symptom formation. Starting at the bottom, first the organic factor (irritation of the throat), its suscep-tibility to fixation as an erotogenic zone; second the role of identification, specifically with her father; then determinants from the Herr K. object relation, and lastly the symbolic link-age of dyspnia and the sounds of sexual intercourse. The link between leucorrhea, vaginal discharge, and vaginal lubrica-tion as excitement bears on the disgust Dora remembered as her affect on being kissed by Herr K. Freud is aware of the deficiencies in his formulation but offers the excuse that ter-mination was premature. Other cases more thoroughly ana-lyzed are more convincing.

When Freud returns to the dream after his neurosogenic detour, he offers us a Zeigarnic Effect theory of recurrent dreams. They have to do with an intention that needs to be carried out but isn't. The dream intention is "I must fly from this house for I see that my virginity is threatened here. I shall go away with my father, and I shall take precautions not to be surprised while I am dressing in the morning." The conflict element in Dora's situation vis-a-vis Herr K., present in her conscious awareness and in the dream as well, is clear. This formulation illuminates Dora's clinical situation, but it does not demonstrate the validity of Freud's fundamental theory of dreams. According to that theory. "A dream is not an inten-tion represented as having been carried out but a wish repre-sented as having been fulfilled, and moreover in most cases a wish dating from childhood." In this last section of the second part of the Dora case, "The First Dream," Freud is intent on supporting his dream theory rather than understanding the case, so he states, but it seems that the latter is accomplished at least as well as the former. The infantile wish represented as fulfilled is Dora's oedipal wish. But Freud insists that the oedipal wish is a defense against Dora acknowledging her love for Herr K. Her love for Herr K. is the locus of her con-flict. Freud writes, "She summoned up an infantile affection for her father so that it might protect her against her present" affection for a stranger. But for us Dora's interest in and involvement with Herr K., an older man, constitutes an inappropriate object choice. She has succumbed to the pressure in adolescence of the revival of childhood oedipal wishes.

It is useful to distinguish between a theory of dreams and a theory of dreaming. Freud's discussion about motive force, entrepreneur, and capitalist has to do more with the psychology of dreaming than the analysis of dreams, Clinically, what is important is not so much the motive force for the dream but the motive force for the patient's neurosis; the conflicting forces that lead to the patient's symptomatology, character psychology, inhibitions, and maladaptiveness. The emphasis has to be on the "fabric of structures" of the neurosis rather than the "fabric of structures" of the dream.

When Freud refers to premature sexual enjoyment, he is again in a seduction theory mode rather on unconscious sexual fantasy and the role of dream analysis in theories as "pathogenically operative" than one that puts a stress on conflict. Freud refers to recovery of childhood memory events. "This function of dreams has withstood the test of time, with the proviso, of course, that events are not just events but also the attendant fantasies, affects, etc."

The final section of Part 2, "The First Dream" was printed as a footnote in editions earlier than 1924. Freud elsewhere has commented on the primary nature of the process of analysis and the secondary status of synthesis. Technically there is a general attitude that analysis is attended to directly; synthesis takes care of itself. But Freud's synthesis, his reconstruction of the dream process and retracing of the dream work is a tour-de-force. He starts at the beginning, the day after the scene in the woods, the day after Dora had noticed that she was no longer able to lock the door in her room. That is the precipitating danger. Freud infers that she must have said to herself, "I am threatened by a serious danger here," and therefore formed the intention not to remain in the house because of the threat of Herr K.'s intrusions; she would go off with her father instead. The conscious wish to go off with her father was capable of forming a dream because, and only because, it found, as Freud puts it, "a continuation in the unconscious." For Freud this is that fundamental day-to-day intentions, wishes, fears, desires cannot make dreams unless they can connect with unconscious childhood intentions. This is why it is said aphoristically that the scene of every dream is one's childhood. Freud continues, "Her intention of flying to her father which, as we have seen, reached down into the unconscious, was transformed by the dream into a situation which presented as fulfilled the wish that her father should save her from the danger." Freud comments that the hostile feelings against her father had to be suppressed but saved for the second dream. The mind is ever alert for the possibility of using recent situations transformed into infantile situations to produce dreams. Every time this can happen, according to Freud, "is a special triumph." In the Dora case we have the felicitous similarity of the current scene of Herr K. at the bedside matched up with the childhood scene of her father at the bedside, waking her up to prevent her from wetting her bed. The dream work gets down into the unconscious. It picks up along the way the concepts of wet, water, wetness, and their opposites, fire and burning. They connect by chance with her father's recent expressed anxiety about the risk of fire. Lo and behold, the dream picture emerges like an image on a negative in developing solution. The power of the word "wet" as a switch word evolves as the connection is made from wet as in bedwetting to wet as in sexual intercourse.

"Wet" is also connected to dirty and includes within that set of ideas the gonorrheal infection, the catarrh, the wish to dirty and the reaction against it. The concern about cleanliness and dirtiness has a firm foothold in Dora's unconscious, given her mother's cleaning neurosis. And introducing mother into the associative nexus also fills out Dora's oedipal constellation: jealousy of mother complements love for father. Freud proposes that pictorial representation is sought for the con-flictual constellation. The image that does service is jewelry, drops, schmuck. Drops now succeeds wet as the dream switch word. Now with two verbal bridges, Freud tells us, the dream can connect in Dora's mind ideas of her parents' sexual inter-course, her mother's gonorrhea, and her "tormenting passion for cleanliness." But there is a slight hitch. The jewelry image is removed; it has unconscious representation but no day res-idue pull. A simple substitution of jewel case for jewelry does the trick. Herr K. had never given her jewelry, but he had given her a case.

That is the origin of the specific dream image, the jewel case. Freud conveys his sense of delight and marvel at the ingenu-ity of the dream work, which equates jewel case and female genital. "Jewel case," says Freud, "is an innocent word but also one admirably calculated both to betray and to conceal the sexual thoughts that lie behind the dream."

The jewel case is the crown jewel of Freud's interpretation of Dora's dream and of the understanding of her neurosis. The convergence of childhood and contemporary sources, the operation of the mechanisms of condensation and dis-placement and multiple function are all evident. The jewel case represents an oedipal conflict in both its childhood and adolescent versions. Freud faults himself for not pur-suing Dora's father's spoken words in the dream. "I refuse to let my children go to their destruction," or to be more precise "I refuse to let myself and my children be burnt for the sake of your jewel case." But it should be noted that Freud's principle about spoken words in dreams, that they always come from actual speeches, is not universally sup-ported at this time. Freud may have been aware of this when he states, "The result of my inquiry would no doubt have shown that the structure of the dream was still more com-plicated." He implies that behind the remembrance of an actual speech in a voiced unconscious fantasy might lurk.

Freud concludes this section by considering why Dora's

dream recurred at this point in the treatment. Freud is at the edge of recognizing the contribution of the transference to the dream repetition. The dream was a premature termination dream. Dora was getting ready to flee Freud just as she had fled from Herr K. The extent to which Freud was a seducer like Herr K. is something that will require further discussion.

The Dora Case—A Case Of Hysteria—III—The Second Dream

This section of the paper provides us with illustrations of two uses of the dream in clinical practice. The first has to do with its role in the analysis of a symptom; the second its role in the recovery of forgotten memories. These two "successes," psychoanalytically speaking, are presented in the context of analytic failure, as Freud tells us that as soon as the second dream is made intelligible, the analysis is broken off. This outcome is not expected. Freud does not describe his patient at this point as being in a state of significant resistance; in fact, to the contrary, he describes her as being self-reflective. "For some time, Dora herself had been raising a number of questions about the connection between some of her actions and the motives which presumably underlay them." Freud says that he will present the material produced in the analysis of the dream in a somewhat haphazard order, although in actuality he begins with the analysis of the first part of the dream.

He is able very readily to elucidate the day residue and to transform the dream images from indifferent pictures into a scenario in which his patient has a clear role. The subject matter is elevated from a trivial concern with difficulties encountered by a sightseer and a tourist in a strange town to a concern of higher human import, man's quest for woman. Additionally, Freud is able to move the dream from geography to anatomy. The chain is from station to box to women. The pattern of working together that Dora and Freud establish is for Dora to provide the day residue and associations and for Freud to make the symbolic leap from box to female genital, from key to male genital. Should we fault Freud in regard to this aspect of his technique? I think this question can only be answered in context.

One does get the impression that Freud is as intent on analyzing the dream and unlocking its secrets as he is on understanding his patient. There is a means/end issue here. However, at least at this point in the narrative, Dora does not seem to be feeling misunderstood because of Freud's symbolic leaps. On the contrary, she brings forward more material, her associations, recollections, her thoughts, concerns about her father's illness, etc. Perhaps Freud is a little too quick when he "at once" reminds Dora of the farewell letter he had written to her parents, his association to the letter in the dream. Perhaps he might have put it more tentatively or asked her whether or not the letter in the dream called to her mind some other letter. A little bit more tentativeness or hesitation on Freud's part is perhaps in order here, especially in consideration of the fact that Freud moves very rapidly from the letter and its associations and connotations to a core affectively loaded fantasy: Dora's craving for revenge directed against her father. Freud notes that the revenge motif is a new element that has to be taken into account in any "synthesis of her dream thoughts." However, Freud does shift from synthesis back to analysis and with close textual attention, in fact, from a single question mark added after the first telling of the dream, a sign of its importance, as Freud had noted earlier. Freud moves his patient from dream to memory and shifts the scene of the dream from its uncertain location to the by now famous or infamous lake and "the problems connected with it." Freud's approach now is to have Dora give more details about the memory rather than for more associations to the dream. Freud presses on in his inquiry, always looking for specific details and actual words. This is a point of technique that can never be emphasized too strongly. Dora indicates to Freud that he is right in pursuing this particular memory when she recognizes that the wood in the memory, the wood by the shore of the lake, is just like the wood in her dream and is related as well to a recent memory, a picture at an exhibition, and the recent picture, the exhibition picture, includes new elements. Freud is then able in a brilliant leap to translate dream geography into sexual anatomy, or as he puts it, "the symbolic geography of sex." And the geography of sex is the locale for the second fantasy that emerges for Freud in his patient's dreams, namely the fantasy of defloration. To recapitulate, we have uncovered for us by Freud two fantasies: (1) the fantasy of revenge against father and (2) the fantasy of a man forcefully entering a woman's genital. The question as to whether or not these two fantasies are related and whether the man is father and the revenge motif is for such a sexual action is not addressed at this point, but Freud does tell us that he informed Dora of his conclusions at this point and was that a forced entry, we would ask? But Freud offers us another pun, "The impression made upon her must have been forceable," Dora remembers another piece of the dream, "She went calmly to her room and began reading a big book that lay on her writing table," and the last addendum to the dream is, "She saw herself particularly distinctly going up the stairs." Freud tells us that those pieces of her dream that were first forgotten and are only subtly remembered are invariably the most important from the point of view of understanding the dream. So we therefore have to expect that these final addenda will bring us to new and most significant understandings. However, the path that Freud takes us on following Dora is not to further elucidation of the dream but rather to the analysis of a symptom. Freud reconstructs that Dora had read about sexual matters in an encyclopedia, felt guilty about this activity, and gave herself an illness like one she had also read about in its pages. But what about the particular symptom picture and particularly perityphlitis and foot-dragging? Freud is stymied for a little bit but then gets back on track by focusing on details and in this case specifically periods of time. Dora's attack of appendicitis took place nine months after the scene at the lake. The meaning is clear, the symptom is a fulfilled fantasy of childbirth.

This is then fantasy number three, and again one that can also be connected to the first two, childbirth follows defloration and father is revenged upon either for being the perpetrator or for not. The second symptom, foot-dragging, can be easily connected to the first, the connection is linguistic between false step and unplanned-for conception. Freud at this point is not satisfied with what might seem to us to be a credible piece of analytic work. His theory reminds him that he must find some infantile prototype to account for the symptom because, "Recollections derived from the impressions of later years do not possess sufficient force to enable them to establish themselves as symptoms." However, the infantile prototypes that he comes up with are more of an example of somatic compliance than childhood fantasy. Dora obliges him with a memory of having twisted her foot once when she was a child. Freud then gives Dora his "big interpretation," relating the fantasy uncovered by the dream to her feelings and motivations following the scene at the lake.

In this interpretation, which goes on for 14 lines, Freud fulfills the topographic therapeutic dictum, "Where the unconscious was, the conscious shall be," and he indicates that his interpretation is convincing, "and Dora disputed the fact no longer," although he also adds in a long footnote a few "supplementary interpretations" without telling us whether or not these were also offered to Dora at this point. However, Freud tells us that Dora adds a "so what?" to her acknowledgment of the validity of his interpretation, depreciating its significance. Her comment is: "Why has anything so very remarkable come out of it?" We are somewhat prepared but are still surprised by Dora's termination announcement at the beginning of the next session. Freud's response to Dora's termination announcement is to proceed with the analysis and again he focuses on a temporal detail. Dora decided to terminate a fortnight ago. Freud connects "fortnight" to governesses, a "fortnight's warning," and Dora follows along Freud's line of inquiry. One would anticipate that this would not get Freud very far but, lo and behold, Dora's recollection of the governess who had been another lover of Herr K. leads to "a piece of material information coming to light in the middle of the analysis" that helps solve problems that had been previously raised. We have to wonder about Freud's reference to the "middle of the analysis" since this is, as he has told us, the last session, the end of the analysis. However, this provides him with the information he needs to offer to Dora another long interpretation and reconstruction, one in fact that takes 22 lines. Freud tells Dora what she really felt, contrary to what she has maintained. "It was not that you were offended at his suggestion, you were actuated by jealousy and revenge."

Dora does not seem to fight Freud's interpretation but rather just quibbles about one detail. "Then why did I not tell my parents at once?" And, of course, Freud's answer to her question further stresses the point he is trying to make about her wishes in regard to Herr K. Freud unmasks Dora's wish to marry Herr K, Freud puts it all together for Dora in an interpretation that lasts a page. Dora listens to him "without any of her usual contradictions" and says goodbye. Freud finishes his analytic work in the amount of time Dora provides for him, this one last session, and Freud's analytic efforts in this regard seem to leave very little time or room for him to explore his patient's feelings about and feelings at termination. Freud viewed his alternatives in regard to Dora at this point as either to have continued with the analysis as he did or attempted to keep his patient under treatment by "acting a part."

For Freud there was only analytic abstinence or transference gratification and, Freud stresses, Dora's termination at this point was "an unmistakable act of vengeance" just when his hopes of therapeutic success were at their highest. Freud does not consider the possibility that interpretation of this transference might be a third option in regard to this premature termination scenario. Freud ends this third section and the main part of his discussion of his case with a meditation on human conflict and the limitation of the

151

capacity of reality to tame the "demons that inhabit the human breast." And finally, in Freud's final footnote on p. 110, Freud lists all the fantasies that he has implicated in the structure of the dream, including the oedipal one with its aggressive and libidinal components and the negative oedipal constellation (her love for Frau K.).

At Last: Dreams for Controversial Discussions

Arlene Kramer Richards

Why a dream-within-a-dream? Why is a simple dream not enough? Does the duplication reflect duplicity? Is the dreamer hiding behind two screens? What makes the double screen useful?

A dream-within-a-dream is reported by Primo Levi (2015) in his memoir of life after Auschwitz during a long, painful journey back home to Italy after liberation. The journey back was complicated by his Italian citizenship since Italy, in partnership with Nazi Germany, had lost the war. Stranded in Poland, starved, often freezing, sometimes gravely ill, lonely for his home and family, he had lived a second nightmare after the liberation. Hated by the Germans for being a Jew, he was now hated by Poles for being Italian.

On his first night back home, he dreamt a dream that he had many times after that. He writes:

> It's a dream within another dream, varying in its details, unique in its substance. I am at the table with my family, or friends, or at work, or in a verdant countryside—in a serene, relaxed setting, in other

words, apparently without tension and pain—and yet I feel a subtle, profound anguish, the definite sensation of a looming threat. And in fact, as the dream proceeds, little by little, or brutally, each time in a different way, everything collapses and is destroyed around me, the scene, the walls, the people, and the anguish becomes more intense, and more precise. Everything now has turned into chaos; I am alone at the center of a grey and murky void, and, yes, I know what this means, and I also know that I have always known it. I am again in the Lager and nothing outside the Lager was true. The rest was a brief holiday, or a trick of the senses, a dream: the family, nature in flower, the house. Now this internal dream, the dream of peace is over, and in the external dream, which continues coldly, I hear the sound of a well known voice: a single word, not imperious, but brief and subdued. It is the dawn command of Auschwitz, a foreign word, feared and expected: get up "Wstawać." (p. 397–398).

The experience of fear so profound that it is etched in his mind, in his brain, remains with him for life. The contrasting experience of the peaceful inner dream cannot erase it. The trauma of the camp, extended into the trauma of the post camp exile blots out the life he led before and after the traumas. He wakes into fear even as he returns to a peaceful life at home.

In an account of dreams and dreaming from prehistoric times to the present day Sidarta Ribeirra (2021) cites neurological research showing that Freud's understanding of dreams has been confirmed in two important respects: (1) dreams regularly use experiences of the day before the dream as part of the dream narrative; (2) dreams are built on desire, or what Freud called "wish." In addition dreams have been shown to use the past to predict and control future action. By converting present day experience into a network of past memories, they convert short term memories into long term components of the memory system in the brain.

Yesterday I was driving up a quiet street in a small town, following a large truck. Suddenly the truck overturned a tall metal pole close to the curb. As I passed the pole, it seemed to be coming down on the roof of my car. I saw that I could not go faster because the truck was in front of me. There was nothing I could do to avoid an accident. I was helpless. At that moment time seemed to go slower. I saw a vivid image of the engine cover flapping up to completely obscure my windshield. But my image came from a time over fifty years earlier when I had the engine cover of the car I was then driving sixty miles an hour open on a highway in Virginia. I had taken my foot off the gas, but did not turn or brake so that I came to a slow and safe stop. That time I had made my peace with the idea that I could die then and there. As I came to a stop, I appreciated the good life I had until then. The pole fell inches behind my back bumper.

Afterward, it seemed to me that the image of the blind wind-shield was a defense. It was telling me that I had gotten through worse, that I could make it through now. I thought of a paper by Ernest Kafka about examination dreams and his interpretation that such dreams were a defense against current fears that worked by reminding the dreamer that she had passed such examinations in the past.

Does such an understanding of dreams as reassurance fit with Freud's original idea that all dreams are wish fulfillments? I think that it is a wish for safety that such dreams are depicting. This fits with the idea that nightmares are also wish fulfillments. When one wakes up after a nightmare, there is a sense of relief that the horror either did not happen, or is in the past. The conscious manipulation of recurrent nightmare dreams that some therapists recommend serves to reinforce the idea that nothing so bad will happen in the present or the future (NPR).

If dramatic dreams are failures to master previous drama, having a dream-within-a-dream is a good way to add an extra layer of reassurance to the dreamer. If it is only a dream and the dreamer realizes this even in her sleep, the dream about a trauma is not necessarily traumatic in itself. It becomes benign by being doubly sequestered from waking rationality.

References

Levi, P, (2015). *The Complete Works of Primo Levi.* New York: Liveright.

Ribeirra, S. (2021). *The Oracle of Night: The History and Science of Dreams.* New York: Pantheon.

About the Contributors

Charles Fisher, MD, is a Training and Supervising Analyst at the San Francisco Center for Psychoanalysis and a Personal and Supervising Analyst at the Psychoanalytic Institute of Northern California. He is Deputy Director of the Science Department of the American Psychoanalytic Association and Chair of the Research Grants Subcommittee of the International Psychoanalytical Association. Along with his colleague, Beth Kalish, he has studied dreams and dream interpreting practices among the Achuar people, an indigenous group in the Amazon Rainforest in Ecuador and Peru. *Amazon Dreaming* is the title of a forthcoming book by Fisher and Kalish.

William Fried, PhD, is neither a scientist nor a conquistador although he was elected to the society of Sigma Xi, the scientific honor society, on the presumed scientific merits of his doctoral dissertation, and he once aspired to become a bullfighter. Both occurred early in his career, the bullfighting enthusiasm late in his teens, and the Sigma Xi honor on attaining his PhD. In his time, he has been a very good teacher, and he has more recently overcome some of the most stubborn impediments to becoming a good psychoanalyst. He has written about these and other matters, but his only book is a psychoanalytic examination of movies. It is titled *Critical Flicker Fusion: Psychoanalysis at the Movies.* It is a good book and deserves more readers than it has had.

Fried is a photographer. He had three solo shows, the last several years ago. He still takes pictures, but they are in his computer, not displayed publicly. He had 12 years of experience as an officer of psychoanalytic organizations and left without looking back.

William Fried reads and writes poetry as well as memoirs. He wonders whether the time will come when the memoirs, poetry, and other candid writings by psychoanalysts will appear regularly in Pep Web listings. Apropos that thought, he recalled that one of his poems that appeared in a psychoanalytic journal is already cited and recoverable in Pep Web.

Eugene Mahon, MD, is a training and supervising psychoanalyst at the Columbia Center for Psychoanalytic Training and Research. He has published many articles on a great diversity of psychoanalytic issues. His most recent book *Such Stuff As Dreams* (IPBooks 2022) was also published in Italian as *La Sostanza dei Sogn.*

Edward Nersessian, MD, is a member of the New York Psychoanalytic Institute and Society and training and supervising psychoanalyst. He has written on Curiosity and its role in psychoanalytic technique; on "re-evaluating Freud's basic tenets; On conflict theory and on dreams amongst other subjects. He is currently the director of the Helix Center for Multidisciplinary Studies.

Arlene Kramer Richards, EdD, is a psychoanalyst and a poet. She is a Training and Supervising Analyst with the Contemporary Freudian Society and the International Psychoanalytic Association and Fellow of IPTAR. She is currently faculty at the CFS and Tongji Medical College of Huazhong University of Science and Technology

at Wuhan, China. Her education at the University of Chicago introduced her to the dialogues of Plato. That gave her a sense of what she now think of as her calling. Talking with people who are willing to learn her truth and teach her theirs has been the theme of her professional life. Psychoanalysis gave her her voice and focused her listening. It made excellent use of her curiosity and her love for teaching others. She especially enjoy conversations with ancient authors, feeling like a time traveler in conversation with the past.

Arnold D. Richards, MD, was Editor of *JAPA* from 1994 to 2003 and, prior to that, Editor of *TAP.* He is a member of the Contemporary Freudian Society and an honorary member of the American Institute for Psychoanalysis. He published a series of five volumes of his selected papers *Volume I: Psychoanalysis: Critical Conversations, Volume 2: Psychoanalysis: Perspectives on Thought Collectives, Volume 3: The Psychoanalyst at Work, Volume 4: The Peripatetic Psychoanalyst, and Volume 5: The World of Psychoanalysis and Psychoanalysts.* He also wrote a memoir, *Unorthodox: My Life in Psychoanalysis,* and he has co-edited four books. With Arlene Kramer Richards, he has founded and taught a psychoanalytic teaching program at the Mental Health Hospital in Wuhan, China and is receiving an award from the hospital and municipality in Wuhan this spring. Dr. Richards is the publisher of internationalpsychoanalysis.net

Arnold Rothstein, MD (1936-2022), taught psychoanalytic theory and technique for more than forty-five years. In addition he published four books: *The Narcissistic Pursuit of Perfection, The Structural Hypothesis: An Educational Perspective, Psychoanalytic Technique and the Creation of Analytic Patients* and *Making Freud More Freudian;* edited

seven more; and published numerous scientific papers. He was past Chair of the Program Committee of the American Psychoanalytic Association, past Program Chair for North America of the International Psychoanalytical Association, and past Director of the Institute for Psychoanalytic Education affiliated with the New York University Medical School.

Brent Willock, PhD, studied psychology at McGill University, then earned his doctorate in clinical psychology from the University of Michigan. After several years in the Department of Psychiatry at the University of Michigan Medical Center, he relocated to Toronto, becoming Chief Psychologist at a clinical facility associated with the University of Toronto. He was Adjunct Faculty, York University, and Associate Faculty Member, School of Graduate Studies, University of Toronto. He is Past President of the Toronto Institute for Contemporary Psychoanalysis and serves on the Board of the Canadian Institute for Child & Adolescent Psychoanalytic Psychotherapy. He is a faculty member in the Postgraduate Program in Psychoanalysis and Psychotherapy at Adelphi University's Derner School of Psychology, Writing Mentor for the Washington Psychoanalytic Foundation's New Directions in Psychoanalytic Thinking Program, Associate Editor for *Psychoanalytic Dialogues,* and has contributed many book chapters and articles. He is the author of *Comparative-Integrative Psychoanalysis,* and *The Wrongful Conviction of Oscar Pistorius,* and edited several books that received Gradiva and Goethe Awards. His many contributions have been honored by the Ontario Psychological Association, the American Psychological Association, the Canadian Psychological Association, the International Federation for Psychoanalytic Education, the University of Chicago, the Chicago Institute for Psychoanalysis, and the National Association for the Advancement of Psychoanalysis.

www.ingramcontent.com/pod-product-compliance
Lightning Source LLC
Chambersburg PA
CBHW060231030426
42335CB00014B/1409